Ways of the Hand

Ways of the Hand

The Organization of
Improvised Conduct

David Sudnow

The MIT Press
Cambridge, Massachusetts
London, England

Third printing, 1999
First MIT Press edition, 1993

Printed and bound in the United States of America

Library of Congress Cataloging-in-Publication Data

Sudnow, David.
    Ways of the hand : the organization of improvised
conduct / David Sudnow. — 1st MIT Press ed.
        p.   cm.
    Originally published: Cambridge, Mass. : Harvard
University Press, 1978.
    Includes bibliographical references.
    ISBN 0-262-69161-2 (pbk.)
    1. Improvisation (Music)   2. Hand.   3. Jazz—
Instruction and study.   4. Phenomenology.   I. Title.
MT68.S89   1993
786.2'165193—dc20   92-34315
                                              CIP
                                              MN

For
Harvey Sacks
(1935-1975)

Acknowledgments

I would like to especially thank David Belknap, Michael Butler, Emanuel Schegloff, and James Schenkein for the hours of talk we had together. Each in his own way contributed to the development of my thoughts about music making, and each put up with my many false starts with much-needed encouragement.

James March and Michael Cole were particularly instrumental in my research, for they were central in establishing a most extraordinary setting for interdisciplinary work: the School of Social Sciences at the University of California, Irvine. Here an anthropologist could teach a course by having Mexican craftsmen build a boat with the students; a mathematician could explore learning by establishing a school on a farm near the campus; a sociologist could conduct a course whose exclusive focus would be on the opening several seconds of a single conversation; and when they asked me what I could use in my laboratory when a new building was planned, I said that a piano would be nice, and they got me one, to aid my teaching and research in sociology. Without Irvine in the late 1960s, my work would have been impossible. University life everywhere would profit if there were more people like March and Cole.

I owe to Dick Powell, a superb pianist, friend, and critic, the wonderful joys of being able to make music.

Three people participated in my intellectual life with an order of influence to which I hope this study in some measure does justice. Harold Garfinkel provided the impetus for this investigation, in his writings, lectures, and the conversations we had over the years. He pushed me at every point to go for the detailed looks of things; even the most passing comments he made on many occasions revealed an expanding richness of implication as I wrote; his encouragement enabled me to realize the consequences of allowing the keyboard, and not an academic discipline, to tell me where to go. If my study helps to realize the vision of a rigorous ethnomethodology, I would be most pleased.

Harvey Sacks, whose work is well known, was a model for what close thinking, a love of detail, and a commitment to caretaking could be all about as a style of living and working. He was my mentor and friend for fifteen years, and like all those who were so very fortunate to have known him, life will simply never again have the fullness that Harvey made possible. His loss drains me each day.

Robert Epstein, first as an undergraduate student of mine and then as a friend and colleague, discussed every aspect of this study with me in detail, read and reread every page, made suggestions of fine intricacy at each turn, and taught me a great deal about writing. I hope I can one day repay the debt I owe him when it comes time for him to do that masterful work we can surely expect in the future from an extraordinary thinker.

Joyce Backman, of the Harvard University Press, worked terribly hard to see this book through the various stages necessary to reach publication. Her encouragement, editorial help, and support are deeply appreciated.

My children Jessica and Paul, my parents Estelle and Irving—they suffered with me, because of me, and brought special pleasures that sustained me through years of hacking away at the piano and typewriter. I hope I have brought some music into their lives in return.

The hand reaches and extends, receives and welcomes—and not just things: the hand extends itself, and receives its own welcome in the hands of others. The hand holds. The hand carries. The hand designs and signs, presumably because man is a sign . . . the hand's gestures run everywhere through language, in their most perfect purity precisely when man speaks by being silent. And only when man speaks, does he think—not the other way around, as metaphysics still believes. Every motion of the hand in every one of its works carries itself through the element of thinking, every bearing of the hand bears itself in that element.

Martin Heidegger

Preface

From an upright posture I have looked down at my hands on the piano keyboard for some years as I studied jazz music, and when I regard my hands now, my looking is deeply informed by the history of looking I have done.

If I watch my hands on a typewriter, I don't recognize their movements. I am startled by the looks of my hands while typing, just as I'm surprised by the sight of my profile when surrounded by mirrors in a clothing store. It's like witnessing an interior part of my body going through some business.

But the sight of my piano-playing hands is familiar. I know their looks, not only in those intimate ways in which we all know our hands' looks, but as my jazz-making hands. It is the ways of the hand that I watch now. For a long time in learning to play jazz piano, I was busy watching my hands and the terrain of the keyboard to see that they did not get into trouble; or I was looking at the keyboard in order to find places to take my fingers, so that instructional work was occurring as a form of guidance in which my looking was very much implicated. Then my look became preoccupied in more subtle ways, party to a kind of imaginary conceiving of various aspects of the territory in which I was moving. Even when looking away from the keyboard, I would conceive visual 'gestalts' of pathways for use as I was playing. Many jazz students spend a good deal of time approaching the task of improvisation by formulating and using rules, such as various scales, to find appropriate ways for going ahead with the music. It's almost as if you learned to keep on typing by using a rule like this: play every other key on the middle bank of characters; either go up, or down, up a bit then down a bit, up a bit then down a bit then up a bit more, and so on. You would get: *adg dgj dgjl dgjljgd*—hardly an acceptable use of the typewriter.

A layman might not detect that improvised music is not being made as the beginner utilizes such defined routes to locate places to go, especially if the pianist gains facility and fluency in their use. But musicians know it is not jazz—and the beginner knows it too. Still, the pathways are useful. They give you 'somewhere' to be going (without telling you how to go places), and it is important to know where you are going in order to get there correctly, without tripping up along the way, hitting two keys at the same time because of an uncertainty about where to take your fingers, for example. And when you make music, you are obliged to keep on doing work with your hands. You can't stop for long and think through a next place to go. You have to keep on playing. The pathways are useful devices to keep the action going.

For a long while, I guided my hands through the terrain of the keyboard by moving my fingers along the various routes and scales I had conceived. My looking, even when directed at the keyboard after looking was not especially necessary to follow the paths, was so involved in the style of activity under way that I didn't see my fingers' doings as I now see them. The doings were different, and the lookings, 'inside or outside,' were different, for together they were part of a way of proceeding other than what I do now. I am not using pathways to make up melodies. Now I find places to go in the course of going to them, each particular next place at a time, doing improvisation.

From an upright posture I look down and see

my fingers, and my looking is so differently related
to the work of the fingers, in contrast to former
modes of 'hookup,' that I see things I never saw
before, because these happenings never occurred
before. I see my hands for the first time now as
'jazz piano player's hands,' and at times, when I
expressly think about it, one sense I have from my
vantage point looking down is that the fingers are
making the music all by themselves. As I watch the
letters coming up on the page when typing rapidly
along, thinking the thought as my typing, as I
watch the thought seeming to settle down on the
page as the competent flycaster smoothly sets a
lure gently down on a trout pond, I wonder, had I a
similar historical access to the looks of my fingers
at this typewriter keyboard, would I see 'fingers
doing thinking'?

My hands have come to develop an intimate
knowledge of the piano keyboard, ways of exploratory engagement with routings through its spaces,
modalities of reaching and articulating, and now I
choose places to go in the course of moving from
place to place as a handful choosing. In this book,
I want to offer a close description of the handicraft
of improvisation, of the knowing ways of the jazz
body. I want to review the acquisition of jazz
hands, on the way toward the closer study of the
human body and its works: in jazz piano playing
we have an occasion of handicraft of elaborate,
elegant dimensions, a fitting place to explore perhaps our most distinctly human 'organ.'

My concern is description and not explanation, a phenomenologically motivated inquiry into
the nature of handwork from the standpoint of the
performer. Can the body's improvisational ways be
closely described from the viewpoint of the actor,
not through an introspective consciousness, but by
a fine examination of concrete problems posed by
the task of sustaining an orderly activity, which
'improvisation' certainly is? This question sets the
tone of my discussion.

My account is addressed to artists, craftsmen, philosophers, musicians, scientists, and writers, 'professionals' or not, to all who might find a characterization of the hands at work germane to clarifying the nature of the human body and its creations.

The detailed description of mundane experience (which I think is requisite to any carefully controlled study of bodily conduct) is a task whose dimensions are not clearly conceived, despite hearty programmatic calls for the necessity of the effort. The problems of such description—what counts as 'mundane,' what adequate description entails, how description undermines the mundane, and more—are compounded here by my concern to approach adequate description in a specialized realm of activity. To restrict the account to musicians would defeat my interest in offering a sample of a style of descriptive inquiry to students of behavior. To gloss the musical details for the sake of readier accessibility, on the other hand, would not direct attention to the looks of handwork in particular, and if an attempt at a productional account of action is to be successful, leading to the looks of things, then fine details must be had.

So I have tried to make the discussion both accessible and minute at the same time, building a specialized language to deal with an uncharted territory. It makes for a somewhat difficult book. Problems of staying with the discussion as it proceeds can be substantially minimized if the reader briefly 'rehearses' the various critical keyboard examples, using, say, a tabletop to help concretize them. If such simulation is at least attempted, one with no keyboard or musical experience will find the discussion manageable.

Contents

Beginnings

When I went for piano lessons this time around, it was with a determination to understand and accomplish improvised jazz. A dozen years earlier some lessons had amounted to pretty much nothing. A good pianist but poor teacher would have me watch him play a ballad, pausing as he struck each chord, and with a notation system I worked out for myself I wrote down the names of the notes under each finger, then went home and duplicated the songs. I gained a little repertoire of tunes this way, but I didn't know what I was doing: I couldn't improvise, play other songs or the ones I learned in any other way, or teach another to do what I did without using the same method of instruction. I played these songs rather well, however, having a flair for them and a decent sense of music.

My new teacher asked me to show him what I could do with the instrument. I played through some of my rote-learned tunes, practiced the night before (which formed the total basis for the little playing I had done throughout college and the years afterwards), explained how they were acquired, and demonstrated by playing some scales that I could move about the keyboard with facility. I knew how to place my fingers properly, how to engage in some maneuver once it was pointed out to me, and to do so more or less quickly and smoothly. Childhood skills acquired with extensive classical music lessons had not been lost, and in fact my hands had a professional look and manner to them, even though I did not know how to have them do very much. The things they could do they did with the looks of nearly full-fledged pianist's hands. When not doing much, they looked the part.

As a result of my technical ability, this lopsidedness between what my hands could in principle and in fact do, the course of my instruction over the first several months went quite smoothly, and after seven or eight months of extensive daily practice I briefly held a job with a bass player in a yacht-club dining room. Doing jazz improvisation correctly, however, was another matter.

My beginning piano lessons entailed the acquisition of working ability with a host of concepts about the keyboard. In order to play jazz I had to learn about what a 'song' was, what 'chords' were, and how chords could be located and produced on the keyboard. I was told that once the production of chords and songs was mastered, the work of improvisation could be approached, that there would first be this performance device, the full-blown song from front to finish, and it would serve as a format for getting to jazz improvisation

For the jazz musician the song is spoken of as a sequence of chords with an originally written melody, which in garden-variety play is performed through a first time and then the chords are successively reiterated as improvised melodies are substituted for the theme of the tune. When the jazzman improvises, with the exception of practices in so-called free music, he 'plays on the changes,' generates 'melodies laid over' the underlying sequence of chords. When several musicians perform together, they gear their respective actions by employing the same tune, the successively repeated cycle of chords and metrical structure to keep them on the track together, and when musicians take turns in soloing, each managing a bit of the play and giving a next section over to his fellows, the song furnishes a formal organization, a series of benchmarks that delineate turn-taking sections and unify the ensemble's concerted progress.

I ask nonmusician readers to peruse the following quick sketch of 'music theory.' It need not be memorized, reading it straight through will suffice, and should later descriptions be in any way vague, the reader can of course go back over it to refresh his grasp. Don't be concerned about what the structures described here sound like; a rough visual appreciation of the keyboard is needed; those already familiar with the piano, chords, the song chart, and scales should go on to p. 8.

1. Scales

The keyboard is composed of groups of black and white notes, with alternations of two and then three black-note ensembles. Distances between keys are as follows: from any key to the immediately adjacent higher (to the right, of higher pitch) or lower (to the left, of lower pitch) key is referred to as a *half step*. Two half steps comprise a *whole step*. Here are some half steps: 1 to 2, 4 to 5, 5 to 6, 12 to 13. Some whole steps: 1 to 3, 5 to 7, 8 to 10, 11 to 13, 12 to 14:

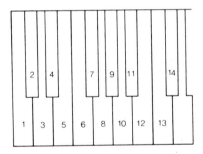

The so-called major scale is a central device in all western music, a sequence of eight notes constructed according to this formula:

$$1 \quad 2 \quad 3 \quad 4 \quad 5 \quad 6 \quad 7 \quad 8$$
$$1 \quad 1 \quad \tfrac{1}{2} \quad 1 \quad 1 \quad 1 \quad \tfrac{1}{2}$$

Starting on any key, a major scale is formed by proceeding from the starting point one whole step up to the second note, a whole step to the third, half to fourth, and so on.

The eighth note of the major scale is considered the same note as the starting note, either one octave higher or one octave lower. Within the scope of one octave range, there are twelve possible starting notes, and thus twelve major scales.

In musical nomenclature, alphabet terms are assigned the notes on the piano:

1. The white notes are named by the terms A through G, duplicated through successive octaves.

2. Black notes are named by reference to the adjacent white notes, a black note termed a 'flat' when named by reference to that white note a half step above it, or a 'sharp' relative to that white note a half step below. The black notes thus take either of two names (this may also be true of white notes, in certain circumstances):

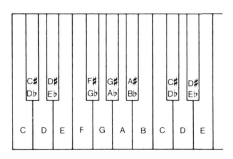

Each major scale is 'spelled' by assigning letters to its notes according to a convention that minimizes awkwardness of nomenclature.

Summarizing, we have twelve major scales, one starting on each of the twelve notes within the scope of the octave, named and comprised as follows:

C major: C D E F G A B C
Db major: Db Eb F Gb Ab Bb C Db
       (or C#, which I shall not bother spelling)
D major: D E F# G A B C# D
Eb major: Eb F G Ab Bb C D Eb
E major: E F# G# A B C# D# E
F major: F G A Bb C D E F
F# major: F# G# A# B C# D# E# F#
G major: G A B C D E F# G
Ab major: Ab Bb C Db Eb F G Ab
A major: A B C# D E F# G# A
Bb major: Bb C D Eb F G A Bb
B major: B C# D# E F# G# A# B

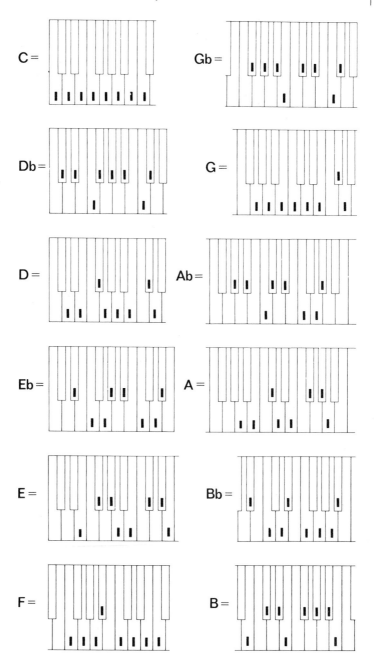

2. Chords

A chord is a group of two or more notes sounded simultaneously. There are three basic chord types: MAJOR, MINOR, and DOMINANT. With few exceptions, all the chords used in jazz music (and most other styles) are of these types. The chords are characterized in terms of the major scale, on the basis of which they are constructed. The major chord is composed of the 1st, 3rd, and 5th notes of the major scale. For example, a C major chord has the notes C, E, and G:

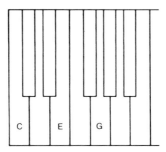

The minor chord is constructed of the 1st, flatted 3rd, and 5th notes of the major scale. C minor: C, Eb, G:

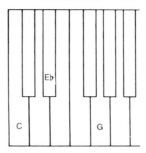

The dominant chord is constructed by adding on to the major chord the flatted 'seventh' note of the major scale. C dominant is C, E, G, Bb:

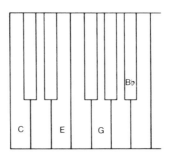

There are twelve major, minor, and dominant chords, each
named by reference to that starting note and major scale
upon which it is constructed.

Chords may be produced in varieties of ways. They may
be inverted, played in various positions on the keyboard (C, E,
G, going from left to right, or E, G, C; G, C, E) and, as is common in modern music, numerous additional tones may be
added to the basic chord constituents to provide for a fuller
sounding structure. Jazz musicians seldom play chords as
specified above, but add various tones to each chord type to
enrich their texture. The particular manner in which a chord is
actually executed on the piano is referred to as the chord's
voicing. Such considerations need not be explored here.

3. Songs

In jazz play, the song is used as a basic formatting device. A song is a more or less fixed pattern of chords, with a
written melody, laid out in a metrical structure, with so many
beats, in an evenly articulated pulse, organized into a set of
measures, groups of accented pulses: **1** 2 3 **1** 2 3 **1** 2 3 or
1 2 3 4 **1** 2 3 4, etc. Most popular songs have standard for-
mats, and tunes with 12, 16, 24, 32, and 36 measures are most
common. Here is a 'chord chart' for a typical standard tune:

"Tenderly"

/Eb	/Ab7	/Ebm7	/Ab7	/
/Fm7	/Db7	/Eb	/Eb	/
/Abm7	/Fm7	/Abm7	/Dm7G7	/
/Cm7	/F7	/Fm7	/Bb7	/
/Eb	/Ab7	/Ebm7	/Ab7	/
/Fm7	/Db7	/Eb	/Eb	/
/Abm7	/Dm7G7	/Cm7	/Am7D7	/
/Gm7C7	/Fm7Bb7	/Eb	/Eb	/

The song chart, without a notated melody (the symbols desig-
nate the chords as major, minor, or dominant), here furnishes
a diagram of the harmonic structure of "Tenderly," written in
the key of Eb Major. This essentially means that most of the
melody notes are chosen from the notes of the Eb Major
scale. The song can be played in any of the twelve keys. Each
measure takes three beats, this tune written in so-called waltz
time.

Each song has a more or less unique harmonic structure,
but the progression of chords, one to the next, follows certain
principles of chordal movement, so that common patterns of

progression are found in all tunes. There are rules for 'chord - changes, not necessary to explore here, such that nearly every popular song's harmonic structure is fundamentally similar, each with only slight variations from others. A musician with experience with many songs learns these common harmonic patternings, and one with experience comes to find appropriate chords to 'harmonize a melody' in fairly short order, given recurrently used patterns of movement through courses of changing chords.

There are various ways of speaking about the relationships obtaining between a melody and an appropriate 'chordal harmonization,' ways of musicologically speaking that need not concern us here, such relations to be discussed in quite different terms in due course.

In my early lessons, principles of chord construction and 'voicing,' manners of producing the chords in pleasingly textured and located ways on the keyboard, were the main topics of study. However a chord may be described in terms of its theoretical organization as a constellation of named notes, located on a keyboard with geometric and measured properties, in song play a chord is a grabbed place. What is involved in chordal place grabbing?

Anyone who has witnessed or been a beginning pianist or guitarist learning chord production notices substantial awkwardness. A good deal of searching and looking is required at the outset. The chord must be detected, first seen as a sequence of named notes taken in with a look that reviews the terrain up and down, finding the chord as a serial ordering of these and those particularly identified tones, going from left to right or right to left, consulting the rules to locate places. Then some missing ones in the middle are filled in. And along with such looking are hands that behave correspondingly.

I found a particular chord, groping to put each finger into a good spot, juggling around the individual fingers a bit to find a nice way to get the hand arranged so that it felt comfortable, and once having a hold on the chord, getting a good grasp, I

would let it go, then look back to the keyboard |
only to find that the grasp had not yet been properly established. It was necessary to take up the
chord again in terms of its constitution, to find the
individual notes again, building it up from the
scratch of its spoken parts. Over the course of my
first hours and days, much time was spent doing
initial grabbing, trying to get hold of the chords
properly, going back and looking at them constitu-
tively as named notes, grabbing again, reposition-
ing the hand to get into the chord with a comfortable hold, so that the chord could be grasped as a
whole; finding ways of sinking into the chord that
did not involve production of neighboring tones;
arching the hand appropriately so that the fingers
came down with the correct spacing and trajectory
relative to the shape of the chording hand; balan-
cing the different intensities of pressure so as to
not lose balance, the edges of neighboring notes
coming to be encountered not as extraneous edges
to be avoided but edges whose tactile appreciation
became part of the hold on the settled-into chord;
arching the hand and arraying the fingers with the
sort of proportional spreading that, when the chord
was reached for, the fingers not only came into the
right spots but with equal intensity, so that the
tones all sounded homogeneously and not clumsily
serialized, like the poor high-school band serializes
the voices of an opening chord in the marching
tune.

As my hands began to form constellations, the
scope of my looking correspondingly grasped the
chord as a whole, a consistency developed in seeing not its note-for-noteness, but the pattern of its
location as a configuration emerging out of the
broader visual field of the terrain. Looking's work
became expansive in scope as the reaching was
concurrently moving for constellations. Sitting at
the piano and moving into the production of a
chord, the chord as a whole was prepared for as
the hand moved toward the keyboard, and the ter-

rain was seen as a field relative to the task. The keyboard is as many sorts of places as there are activities to be undertaken with it, a rather different-looking place to the cleaning lady than to the musician who in the course of play may see past it into the music with a look that is hardly looking at all.

It is not enough for song production to know how to get into a chord. Getting into and out of chords, from one then on to the next, becomes essential, and a host of expanding skills, ways of looking, moving, reaching, and thinking, must be developed to execute correct successions of chords. For me, it was only a short time before individual chords were properly grabbed places, and in a couple of weeks I could smoothly produce all the dominant, major, and minor chords in the voicings taught me and with the additional tones jazz players commonly employ. Turning to chord charts, to songs, producing successions of chords became my task.

There was chord A and chord B, separated from one another, this one some distance down the keyboard from the other. A's production entailed a tightly compressed hand, and B's required an open and extended spread. A's production was accomplished by coming at the keyboard straight ahead, as one comes at the typewriter to establish contact with the home position, while B's involved a shift in the axis of the hand relative to the keyboard, with, for example, the little finger having to go farther away from the body's center than the thumb. And A is played for counts 1 2 3 4 and at the time the next 1 arrives, B must be played.

The beginner gets from A to B disjointedly. The grasp of A may be in hand, and B as well, but there is a distance to be traversed, and what happens at first is that after doing A, the novice sets out for B without going for it in the right way from the outset. You move for B, going to the left because it lies below A, but you don't set out for it in

the fashion required, not going for the whole of B. Setting out for B's rough place on the terrain, and getting into its vicinity, it is necessary to configurate for its production. Going correctly from A to B, reaching for the whole of B, is to be directed from the start not merely toward where it is, but to play it on arrival, and that involves preparing along the course of the journey to land in proper productional shape in coming upon the goal. The hand must lift off from A and, as it moves toward B, undergo the appropriate reconfigurations as a smooth course of changing hand shape, one that is not jerky or spasmodic. No sooner does the lift off from A occur than the movement is already toward the all of B, a smooth transition requiring that all necessary adjustments take place simultaneously.

Tempo adherence is a critical resource for such grabbing actions. Having an upcoming time of arrival, pre-established by the preceding beats, 'tells one' when to arrive at B having lifted off A, and as the chording hand moves toward its next destination, the pace of the reconfigurating that brings it down in the next chord position on time is quite obviously given in the tempo of the transition. At fast tempos the shifting shapes occur rapidly and at slow ones the hand aligns gradually.

Smooth chord production for song play must meet additional requirements, for it is not enough to grab chords cleanly, even to move in tempo smoothly from one chord to the next. To play a song well, it must not be necessary to do any more than peripherally monitor the terrain of the keyboard, if at all, to handle chord transactions. At the outset and for a substantial period of time for the beginning piano student, the more so the more complex the chordal structures are and the more rapidly changing the sequence of chords, fairly close surveying of the left-hand side of the keyboard is necessary to negotiate. But before songs can be smoothly played, and especially before improvisatory jazz melodies can be generated, a tilted manner of terrain regard must be overcome.

Looking's workload progressively lightens for finding distances, the gaze at the keyboard progressively diffuses in function, as places gradually become places toward which the appreciative fingers, hand, and arm are aimed. As I reached for chords, and reaching for chords in the song context involves reaching for patterns of chords, for characteristic sequences, I was gaining a sense of their location by going to them, experiencing a rate of movement and distance required at varying tempos, and developing, thereby, an embodied way of accomplishing distances. What 'there' means is how it is to go from place to place as an accomplishment. The symmetricality of the body, and that sort of extensional 'self-consciousness' that enables you to use a toothbrush without monitoring the course of the gesture and without smacking yourself in the face, entails a 'system' with elaborate distancing capabilities.

From the middle of the piano, the beginner gradually acquires an incorporated sense of places and distances, 'incorporated,' for example, in that

finding the named, recognizable, visually grasped
place-out-there, through looking's theoretic work, becomes unnecessary, and the body's own appreciative structures serve as a means of finding a place to go. A grasp of the setting of the keyboard, and its dimensions relative to the hand's and arm's moving extension from the center of the body, develops. In time this skill becomes so elaborated that a precisely maintained alignment from the center point is itself unnecessary.

The advanced pianist needs little bearing in order to reach way out for a particular note, but in ongoing play it is a system of distances that becomes accomplished. Being at this point at the keyboard, having its place at hand and arm, enters into how one goes to some other point, which, from the standpoint of the pianist, is the same as saying where some other point lies.

Only after years of play do beginners attain that sort of full-fledged competence at place finding that the jazz pianist's left hand displays in chord execution. Reaching the point where, with eyes closed, I can sit down at the piano, gain an initial orientation with the merest touch 'anywhere' on the field, then reach out and bring my finger precisely into a spot 'two feet' off to my left, where a half inch off is a mistake, come back up 'seventeen inches' and hit another one, and go down 'twenty-three inches' and get there at a fast clip—a range of skills any competent player has—took a long course of gradual incorporation. Through repeated work in chord grabbing, an alignment of the field relative to the body's distancing potentials begins to take place, and this alignment process varies in delicacy and need in accordance with the form of the music. The rock-and-roll pianist's capacities for lookless left-hand reaching differ from the baroque specialist's, and these both from the stride-style jazz pianist's. Every musical style as the creation of human bodies entails correspondingly constituted tactile facilities for its performers.

To carry on the work of song production with reasonable fluency, attending the various tasks required, some three or four months of practice with many song charts was necessary before I was no longer doing too much looking work in making chord changes for a melody to be well played. By the end of that period I was able to play my growing repertoire of songs without having to regard the left side of the keyboard especially. Playing the full song was relatively easy for me, for finding a melody without a notation at hand was 'unproblematic' (a task considered in detail below). And I had no special difficulty in coordinating the two hands' use, playing a chord every two or four beats, for example, with many more events of varying temporal value sequentially articulated with the right hand. New beginners go through considerable pains over this acquisition.

In several months I could read a chord chart, play the melody of a newly encountered song after a few moments of review, and therefore perform an increasing number of standard tunes with nicely voiced, jazz-sounding chords in correct tempo, with more or less appropriate feeling.

When my teacher said, 'now that you know how to play chords well, why don't you try to improvise melodies with the right hand,' and when I went home and listened to my jazz records, I found that in attempting to make up melodies like that, it was as if the instruction 'go home and start speaking French' had been given.

There was this 'French' going on, streams of fast-flowing sounds rapidly articulated and criss-crossing this way and that, endless sorts of variations, styles within styles in the course of a player's music, with enormous extents of intricate windings about. There were rising and falling intonations, constantly shifting accents, and I was immediately listening in a different way, hearing my records for the first time with a guided interest: how is what I am listening to done?

But it was not entirely 'how is what I am listen-

ing to done?'; it was especially 'how is what I am |
listening to something which I can now set out to do?' That it was done mostly by black men, certainly one way such music was made, was beside the point. That it was done in a musical tradition, with a particular history and evolution of various devices for constructing chords and melodies, mattered only insofar as I had to become involved in that history to do it. That the history entailed increasing demands for technical expertise, corresponding to an increasingly refined instrument for which such technique was geared and from whose aspirations it was fashioned, as well as an increasingly professional position for the musician and the development of an orientation toward the perfect performance, mattered if I had to take up the technical training that much music now played requires. These jazz musicians were doing things very fast. Did my fingers go fast enough? Any theory's relevance depended on its possible bearing for my practicing.

However what may be heard on the records can be described, the first relevant question about this music for me was: 'what notes are they playing?' The music had a rhythm, an assortment of intensities, an intonational structure, subtleties of shading, and more. But when it came to sitting down at the piano, it was a rhythm *of* something, an intensity *of* something, an intonational structure *of* something, subtleties *of* something, and the something that first mattered was: these and those particular notes being played. I could bring my hands to the piano and do 'things' in a jazz rhythm, as I could and did clap my hands to this music for years; I could subtly shade a contact with the keyboard, touching the piano softly, loudly, with delicate nuances in between; I could move my fingers fast or slow. I could do all this as many can do, but the prime question, sitting at my piano, playing a sequence of chords and trying to follow the teacher's instruction to make up melodies with the right hand, was, Where?

It was not anything about what the melodic (right) hand was doing in playing these notes in particular that counted. I did not figure that the looks of the hands could be employed from the outset as guides for learning their doings. When I looked at pianists' hands, I looked past them to the places they were going, not to how they were going about but where. I sat at my piano and had to bring my hands to some particular notes. I could more or less get them to any particular notes I wanted to get them to, given my 'well-trained hands,' but I didn't know which ones to take them to. I learned several years later that where the hands are going very much depends upon how they go about their doings, but the teacher did not tell me about that at the beginning, and doing so would have entailed a much different course of instruction. It seemed most efficacious to approach matters by finding particular places to take my fingers, already knowing how to do that at least in some ways, once places were found. And my teacher encouraged this approach.

I got a first taste for the magnitude of the problems I was in for when I tried to listen to a piece of jazz melody on a record and then go to the piano to play it. I found that while I could perfectly well hear a simple melody a few times over and attain it as a singable accomplishment with voice and hands, these jazz melodies were by no means 'simple.' A three-second stretch of play, within the course of an ongoing jazz improvisation I had listened to for many years, demanded several hours to catch the details sufficiently and bring each of its tones to singability, to get the strip done at the keyboard. The looks alone of a transcription of that much jazz melody are themselves informative:

(Oscar Peterson, "I've Got the World on a String")

Even when taking a portion of a melody from a record where I thought I knew the improvised section well (and it is worth noting that the existence of the recording gives improvised melodies a status they would otherwise not have, that they can be reheard and learned as 'fixed melodies'), a symptomatic vagueness in my grasp of these familiar improvisations was discovered. I knew the melodies only in certain broad outlines. Particularly with respect to the rapid passages, I found that, when singing along with a Charlie Parker recording, for example, I had been glossing the particularities of the notes in many of my hummings, grasping their essential shape perhaps but not singing them with refined pitch sensitivity. It was particular notes that needed to be at hand to reproduce that stretch of music in its particularity, and the question arose: what had I in fact been listening to as a jazz fan all these years?

The extraordinary difficulties I experienced in a first solo-copying attempt, trying to find the tiny spot on the record again and again, endlessly rehearing the same minuscule passage to narrow in on its notes, finding the notes on the piano, working out a fingering solution that did not merely play the right notes but with the right temporal values—these were accompanied by a sense that this was certainly not the way to do it. Moreover, I wanted to be making 'improvised melodies.'

I told my teacher: I don't know where to go, how to start this making up melodies as you go along; tell me where to go. There was no problem in playing several notes over and over again and keeping that up throughout the course of the song cycle, but this clearly was not jazz, any more than noinoinoinoinoinoinoin is English writing, which I can do forever and in various tempos. He of course agreed.

Here was the problem. There is this song, its melody having been played and now to be sustained as a continuing cycle of chords. If I was to do jazz play it was to be playing melodies 'over' these song chords, not just learning this snatch of melody and that one, but playing on the changes for sustained periods of time. The 'changes' keep changing, one must continue play while negotiating the chords at proper places, and my right hand had absolutely nothing to say in this language. It might as well have gone anywhere, but once it did, there was nothing next for it to do, and I discovered from the outset that if you don't know where you are going you can't go anywhere, except incorrectly. The hand had to be motivated to particular next keys to depress, and when there was nowhere for it to go it became totally immobilized, stumbled around, and between 'me' and 'it' there was a rather alienated relationship.

My teacher dealt with my 'where to go' problem by giving me some routes to take. The pathways he gave me, and which I followed in evolving ways over the years to follow, were rather peculiar sorts of routes. He started out by saying, 'with this particular chord you can get a characteristic jazz sound by playing this particular scale.' We looked at a particular chord and then a particular scale, and examined their respective constructions. This is how he spoke of matters:

If you take a 'dominant seventh chord,' for example, say an F dominant:

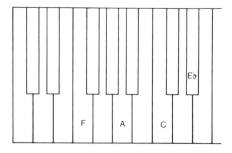

you can play a diminished scale constructed of alternating half steps and whole steps:

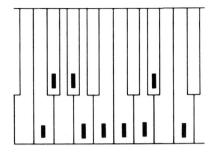

And, he said, you get a 'characteristic jazz sound' arising because of various dissonances that occur when there is the sustained chord's sound coupled with the occurrence of various notes of the scale being played over it. The second note of the scale is a half step above the F of the chord, the third note a half step below the A, the fifth a half step below the C, and the seventh a half step below the Eb. And these half-step dissonant concurrences in particular have a grating sound, a husky, bluesy quality frequent in jazz melodies. But to talk of this 'characteristic jazz sound' is like saying that a sort of broad A is characteristic in Boston speech; being able to produce that sound and having a native conversation in Harvard Square are rather different achievements.

There were, in the case of the diminished scale, which he furnished at first, not one but three versions, depending upon the starting note and whether you count the first step as a whole or a half step. Because of these various dissonant relationships, and relationships between the various chords, the three different diminished scales, he said, each 'go well with' four of the twelve dominant chords. With an orientation to the song and the need to do melodies that accorded with the harmony, having these three scales was to have places to be going with all the dominant chords.

I went home with the step rule written in my notebook, located the three diminished scales, and did what having a linear array almost asked to be done: I learned how to play them fluently as scales, as rising and descending successions of notes. Though he furnished a pathway that was not really a route at all but only a collection of what could be regarded as arrayed places, I took up with it first as a left-to-right and right-to-left sequence of notes. Having now such 'jazz-sounding' places to go, it was of course unavoidably necessary to pick some hows to be going there, and doing scales as scales was a most useful sort of how. I could learn to do them fast and, since they 'duplicate themselves' at successive octaves, there was a long string of action available, starting low and going way up or vice-versa. He had in fact introduced these characteristic jazz sounds by doing just this, showing a scale by playing it as such.

Using the scales involved me in working out 'fingering solutions.' Here is the above diminished scale and that single solution I found best suited to smooth and rapid production, from low to high, over the range of several octaves (1 = thumb, 2 = index finger, 3 = middle finger):

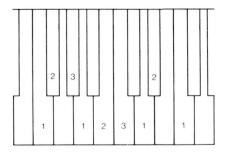

(A slightly different fingering was preferred for a descending passage.)

I worked out fingerings for the three diminished scales, practiced their fluent production as scales, so that in a short while it was unnecesary for me to consider their theoretic constitution. I could produce them rapidly without looking at the keyboard, and I then set about practicing each of the

scales with the appropriately corresponding domi- |
nant chord, type A fitting these four dominants,
type B those, and C the others.

In my first weeks of 'improvisation,' whenever
a dominant chord came up I had a course to take. I
would play one of my diminished scales, characteristically beginning at a place where I could sustain a long run: I would have, say, four beats of
time to fill, with a moderate tempo-ed song some
two or so seconds, and these jazz melodies were
fast so it was the production of a long stretch of
swiftly flowing notes that I wanted.

When a scale was learned at first, I consulted
the rule and regarded the individual notes by way
of it, finding the arrayed course of keys. In short
order a gestalt of the scale as a whole was detected, and I saw the path itself as a figure against
the background of the terrain. But the scale was
detected not merely as a 'scale to be seen,' but a
'scale to be seen and played,' and a starting place
was given special status within the sight. When I
regarded the keyboard to find this diminished
scale, for example, I would see the bounded starting point most prominently; looking down from
above it went from F up to the next F, for how I had
practiced fingering the scale became part of the
way it was visually appreciated.

When I first learned the scales, attention was
given to each note and that finger whose use with
each note produced the most fluent production,
but once this course was mastered, it became a
way of my scale-playing hand, just as chords
passed from being individually fingered into handfully grabbed places. And there were these three
diminished scales to begin with, each identified by
reference to a theoretic system that related its use
to four of the twelve dominant chords, so in my
thinking there was a 'cognitive map,' each scale
named by a starting place, each related to its class
of chords.

I went for each scale at a particular place, a

finger-to-finger orientation supplanted by a whole-handed entry. Having scales available this way made it difficult, at the beginning and in the course of ongoing play, to enter into the scale's production on some note other than the starting note by which it was learned. Only after consider-able practice at upward and downward playing had progressed, did I gain facility entering other points. Consider the diminished scale again:

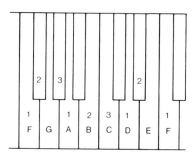

At first, nearly every time, I started on the F with the thumb and rose upwardly; then I came to play it using the fourth finger on the A, coming down with a 3, 2, 1 fingering over the first three notes, and then back up as shown above. With the use of the fourth finger, a rapid downward course from the A and quick turnaround into an upward run was achieved. (Using the thumb on the A, which I employed in a bottom-to-top fingering, was a less fluent way of beginning a downward course for the scale's production.)

Going for this particular diminished scale sel-dom entailed starting on the B with the second finger, for example, not because I couldn't sustain a rapid movement beginning in that position but because, in the way the scale was learned, avail-able as an at-handful rather than individual note-individual finger affair, I did not 'know' that for this scale's production my second finger was used on the B. It was only most initially learned that way, and just as finger-character responsibilities on the

typewriter are forgotten as conceptually available
facts, that finger which played the B in the course
of this particular diminished scale was lost sight of
(when teaching scale fingerings to students today,
I must myself play the scales in order to discover
'best fingers').

My maneuvers with the diminished scale at
first were very limited. Over the course of the first
years of play, nearly everytime I played this particular scale, as one instance, I either started on the F
with the thumb, or on the fourth finger then moving down to the F, this variation my common
negotiation with that routing. In years to come
there were many sorts of manipulations I would
experiment with in the employment of these
scales. Consider the numerical bank of characters
on the upper typewriter range. One may go directly
up, 1234567890; one can go up 123 234 345 456 567
678 789, or 132 243 354 465 576 687 798, or in my-
riad ways. The teacher afforded me only a pathway
and not particular manners for its use, such manipulations as the above common 'order' devices in
melodic work. There are many possibilities more
intricate of course: 1354 2465 3576 4687 . . . 13423
24534 35645 46756 57867 . . . all sorts of elegant
series achieved by maneuvers that employ some
particular order of interdigitation and some intervallic transposition, creating levels of 'orderliness'
by an artful employment of the dextrous hand.

I did not work over these scales in this fashion
from the outset, chiefly because I felt that what
was needed to have at hand was not merely one
pathway to use with a given dominant chord, but a
variety of them. Having learned the three diminished scales, I played them more or less in one or
two first acquired ways, gaining facility at matching them up with their corresponding dominant
chords. Attention was devoted to gaining numerous 'places to go,' practicing various pathways for
the dominant, major, and minor chords, engaging
in an analysis of the keyboard in search of new

routes to take. No matter how many manipulations I performed with a given scale, the use of such a scale was not only something I heard as a constant repetitiveness in my play, but at the same time, and most importantly, I was being encouraged to find other 'solutions' to the various chords. My teacher was preparing me to play jazz music, and jazz music of a particular sort (the 'bebop' tradition with frequently changing chords), and it involved the 'use of' many different sorts of structures rather than a host of manipulations of the above sort on a single-scale device (as in some contemporary forms of improvisatory modal play, which I came to explore only much later).

I went to my lesson each week, my teacher would have me improvise on the chords, and I played little pieces of melody using such first ac-quired scales: up would come this chord and down would go this melody, then a next chord and a scale-like device used for it, then on to the next. It was a terribly awkward procedure at first, for it took some while before my device-selection work became easeful in rapidly picking a run to use with some next chord.

Although my teacher had provided readily accessible instruction on such matters as chord production and voicing, offering constructional rules that were easily followed and produced quick results, when it came to assistance with my im-provisational work the lessons became increasingly less satisfying. I would play for a while and he would offer some advice that struck me at the time as being altogether vague, hardly affording sure guidelines for the week's practice work, like 'try to get the phrasing more syncopated.' But then after I did some playing, producing my halting little mel-odies, chord by chord, run by run, each starting at the same points, each going more or less fast be-cause going more or less fast made them sound 'jazzy' at least, he would then attempt to demon-strate a manner of 'phrasing' by doing some im-

provisation himself. As he was flying over the key- |
board, producing the jazz I wanted so much to be doing, all I could see was that whatever he was talking about in talking about 'phrasing,' he was not simply using the few scalar devices that I had been employing for each of the chord types. He was going many more places over the keyboard, producing all sorts of lines that, as I looked past his hands' ways to the places they were going, revealed gestalt-looking courses. Here was a little downward run I could see was 'orderly,' some sort of intervallically ordered array of notes, as the diminished scale had been.

I would spot him going over what I saw was a course. He would go many places where the courseness in this sense could not be detected, involving intricacies that seemed puzzling, but I figured they were constituted as all the rest, and within his play many little spates of orderly passage could nonetheless be spotted. I would ask 'what was that?' He would say 'what was what?' I said 'that little thing you just did over the G minor chord there.' Now a characteristic 'trouble' occurred, whose significance I did not appreciate at the time and for several years. I would say, 'that little thing you just did on the G minor chord,' and he would have a hard time finding what he had 'just done.' He would at times frankly say, 'I'm not following rules so I don't really know what I just did' (and on other occasions admit, 'I just improvise, I really cannot tell you how, you have to have a feel for it'). I would ask him to play some more, or would try to produce some portion of the happening I had been able to spot in the midst of his playing. Given a piece of some possible orderly array of notes, he would accommodatingly do a jazz-sounding figure employing that array, but it was not the one he had originally done. Those, he found it almost impossible to reproduce after their accomplishment. It appeared that only when an express intention to do some play for its reproduction was entertained in the course of a first production, only then would it be possible for him to reproduce it later.

But the new little thing he would do, when I indicated a possible course I was trying to have him reproduce, was good enough for me, and I would write it down, not necessarily in its details as a notated set of pitches, but by extracting a principle that could be generatively used. For example, he would do some line and then, so as to offer it as an instructable maneuver, we would together speak of its constitution in theoretic terms. I would spot some possibility, he would then take what it appeared I might have been seeing, and do a quick melody which he could then talk of as an arrayed and frozen pathway: 'Well, here, on a dominant chord, you can get a nice sound by playing a major chord arpeggio starting on the second note of the dominant chord's scale.' Having another 'characteristic jazz-sounding piece of melody,' my stockpile increased.

And so it went for a course of some months. I would practice a growing collection of runs, things to do fast jazz melodies with, would spend a short while playing for him at the beginning of each lesson, nervous under his auditing, and he would then do a lot of playing as I spotted 'occurrences' that he then tried to re-create. A negotiation took place over the sorts of things he could extract and give me as principles, a negotiation because at times I got the feeling he was keeping secrets from me. It was like pulling teeth. He would beg off the procedure, offering little in its place, as I would request access to this and that pathway, seeing that he was, after all, taking more routes than I was (though not quite 'taking them'). Reluctantly he would come up with another analysis, giving me an ever-expanding vocabulary of possible words. I acquired an increasing mass of principled solutions for knowing where to go with the various chord types: arpeggios to be taken and scales to be linearly played, various 'licks' constituted by certain

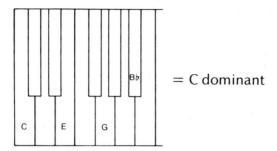 = C dominant

and here, just for the sake of visual appreciation,
are some of the innumerable routes that, produced
more or less evenly and quickly, will yield a 'characteristic jazz sound' with this chord:

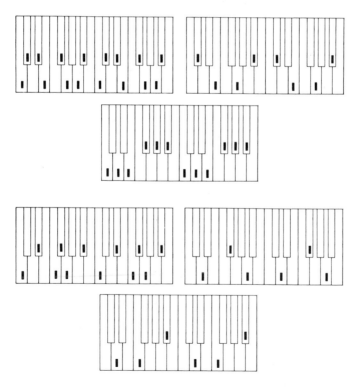

At first the problem of finding somewhere to
go was posed: 'Which notes go well with which

chords?' It became apparent after a while that any of the twelve notes 'can be played' with any of the chords (this so not only for the dominants but the majors and minors as well):

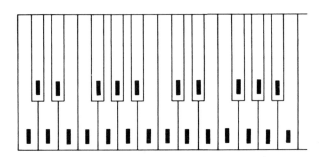

The 'chromatic scale' would itself yield a 'characteristic jazz sound.' Finding that any note would do, however, was tantamount to having no path to take whatever, save the above one.

After about six months of instruction I had: a stockpile of places to go, melodic resources of named notes, these little packages of possibilities, a vocabulary of silent, still sights to be seen, places to go in a theory's terminology on the surface skin of an untouched piano, ways of looking and talking that could be remembered, hosts of licks, written down, told by teachers to students, traded off between students, pieces of professional shoptalk, shopping lists, these routes without speed limits, from no one place in particular to no one place in particular, melodies to be seen at a glance, these wheres without hows, places you can make 'music' with on a wooden, soundless, practice keyboard.

And their use in learning: arrayed places to go, elaborate ranges of possibilities for 'lending organization' to manipulations they themselves told me nothing about, visually detected and then tactilely found fields and criss-crossing vectors for practicing maneuverability with, instantly available potential courses to be seen at a glance while trying to keep up play as the 'changes' went by.

And their use in modes of pathway playing, contrasted with ways of negotiation which in fact make jazz music happen: their utility as the architect's drawing serves the builder in putting up a framing; as the map of a city serves us for knowing what it is to browse, or hurry, or avoid bad neighborhoods, or find our way around the streets in a car when lost, or ride on subways whose entrances are depicted on its intersections; as the rules of chess teach one how to win; as the number of steps from the front door to the corner enables the blind to walk without appearing needful of assistance; as your saying of these sights, *Ya vil gerne ha,* makes you sound Danish (or saying a phonetic version for that matter) and, more than that, having a corpus of such sights provides the ability to have conversation in Tivoli Gardens.

After about six months of instruction and extensive practice with chord charts and my corpus of melody-making equipment, I cultivated opportunities to do some playing with other musicians. I started going to jazz clubs, and became friendly with several members of a circle of players in the community, some of whom were quite accomplished musicians with long experience, and others students in various stages of progress. I wanted to play in a group, and on various occasions I was invited to sit in. In one nightclub in particular, there was a weekly session when musicians from the area would assemble and take turns throughout the evening. There was a bass player and drummer, often several horn players, and musicians would line up for turns, with preferential rights distributed to the better ones first. Novices like myself were given a chance to play a tune or two, and then rather quickly shuffled off the stand. Better players wanted to play with those of their own caliber and the clubowner was concerned to keep 'real music' happening, but beginners were given a chance.

I had learned charts for many of the standard

jazz songs, quite nervously took the stand when invited up for my turn, 'called a tune' to be played, the prerogative of the pianist in a trio situation, established a tempo for the song by calling out a 'one, two, three, four,' as I had seen it done by others, and we were off and running. For me it was as if in a rodeo when the gate opens and the steer takes over.

Recall Charlie Chaplin on the assembly line in *Modern Times:* the conveyor belt continuously comes up, carrying an ever-passing collection of nuts and bolts to be tightened, their placement at regular intervals on the belt, Chaplin holding these two wrenches in his hands, falling behind the time, rushing ahead to catch up, screwing the bolts now faster to keep ahead of the work, missing one or two along the way because the upcoming flow seems to gain speed and he gets frantic, or because it actually does speed up, eventually getting totally caught up in the machinery and then ejected through the factory corridor in a spasmodic, jerky-handed dance.

The music was not mine. It was going on all around me. I was in the midst of the music like a lost newcomer finds himself suddenly in the midst of a Mexico City traffic circle, but with no particular humor in the situation, for I was up there trying to do this jazz I practiced nearly all day, there were friends I had invited to come down with me, and the musicians with whom I had begun to associate.

I was on a bucking bronco of my own body's doings, situated in the midst of these surrounding affairs. Between the chord-changing beating of my left hand at more or less 'regular intervals' according to the chart, the melody movements of the right, and the rather more smoothly managed and securely pulsing background of the bass player and drummer, there obtained the most mutually alienative relations.

I got through the opening sections reasonably

well, playing the song with its originally written
melody, and then came the solo portion. For each
of the now passing chords there would be a pathway selection, and though at home I had achieved
reasonable success at executing these runs
smoothly, under the pressure of the situation they
were very sloppily produced. I played them fast
and there were frequent errors.

The chord lasted for say four beats and the
melody was played rapidly, with two or four or
eight notes for every beat of a four-beat measure.
And now a run for chord A is played, starting near
the middle of the keyboard, and rises up, while the
pathway I knew best for chord B is played starting
at the middle also. So that I started going up with a
fast, sputtering, and nervous scale course, and the
next chord came up and I had to shoot back down
to the middle of the keyboard, to get the thing I
knew how to do well done for it, and then there
was the next chord. My hand jumped around from
place to place like Chaplin stabbing about with his
wrenches. Chords would be missed altogether. I
would draw a blank. An upward-moving line would
more or less end when the chord's sustaining had
to be terminated, no matter where it was. Or, in
order to get to the next starting place, I would end
it a bit sooner, to give myself time to relocate,
feeling the upcoming chord as an encroaching
presence whose necessity was fixed by adherence
to the chord chart of the song we were after all
'playing together,' so that what the left hand was
doing in its pre-set ways was guiding what the right
was then obliged to do. The pacing of the chord
productions would itself become jagged as well,
and I tended to rush the time, changing the chords
a trifle before they were due, or missing a beat here
and there, occasionally having one too many, and
really sweating it out all the way, trying to get
some lines down nicely, checking out the faces in
the crowd and trying not to seem too besieged,

attempting all the while to produce the most intricate of the maneuvers I had learned, to do this full-
blown, fancy, complex jazz those before and after
me in line would do, charging around in the swarm
of the music, trying to 'hold on to the time,' wish-
ing things would suddenly stop for a moment so
that I could catch a breath.

My right hand would become enormously
tired and stiff very soon, and would almost freeze
up, so that while I would struggle to not let errors
occur, where an 'error' meant playing wrong notes
in the course of a path's traverse, there would be
moments when I was simply immobilized and
nothing would come out. Then I would stab for
something else that at home had gone fairly well
but now could not be smoothly taken up the line,
and it would disintegrate.

My 'improvising hand' went not so much for a
sequence of individual tones as for a sight all at
once. The notes of the run were notes to be gotten
over with, the hand setting out on a familiar course
that would not end particularly here or there, but
starting out and keeping up along the route to
wherever it happened to get before the next chord
arrived. The hand set straight out into a course,
going for the whole of it, once committed to its
onset committed to its unaltered continuance as
that course in particular, so that the selection
occurred at the outset and for a while all further
matters were predetermined.

Each of the runs I produced had been more or
less mastered at home, though much less smoothly
done now, and while I could do a good deal of
playing without watching the execution in detail, I
would often watch the course nonetheless, and my
looking or, rather, appealing to the keyboard for
answers, was party to a theoretic in-course analysis I was doing over the keyboard's sights.

But I did not have to always look, for I had
many of the various runs available as tactilely appreciable paths. My looking was occasionally

needed to keep the terrain under regard, to aid large leaps necessary to get from one path onto another, a looking that felt frantic, like searching for a parking place in a big hurry. The music was literally out of hand.

Going for the Sounds

Over the next few years, committed to becoming skilled at jazz, but not tied to the occupation and a need to make a living at it, I played for the most part at home and alone, venturing only occasionally into situations of performance. When I did so, my efforts met with little better success than at first, and I came away from a nightclub or session feeling that my inadequacies were due to a lack of experience and nervousness before others. Although I was advised from time to time to start working as a musician, that by getting a steady job my playing would 'come together,' and while I could see the sensibility of the advice for gaining skills at relaxing in my approach to improvisation, I was not attracted to the work situations someone with my skill level would be at first compelled to pursue. I saw no crucial point at working in noisy bars, where no one seemed to listen to the musicians, when I could play at home, on my own schedule. I had been making what I regarded as real progress on many fronts, sensed that I had a basic grasp over the feelings of what jazz play was like, knew about my play that for all its lacks there was the necessary potential for relevant skills to develop and figured after a year of lessons, with a firm understanding of the theory of the keyboard, chord structure, and melodic principles, I was in position to learn the rest by myself in solitary practice.

I did things for several hours each day that

more or less seemed reasonable. I practiced various technical exercises that I knew all musicians
worked with, spent much time investigating the
keyboard to discover new sorts of melodic configurations, finding various intervallic relationships to
be explored, evolving ever-new pathways constructed on principles similar to ones I had been
instructed about (so that the characteristic jazz
sound was present), listened to a small collection
of records (seldom trying the horrendous task of
solo-copying), and aimed always for what I felt to
be the most sophisticated and intricate examples
of contemporary jazz piano playing. For the most
part, my practice sessions were given over to playing a handful of songs, doing my improvisations.

Fluent manipulations of these pathways produced a semblance of competence, and I was able
to sustain long playing sessions, going for this full-
blown and rapidly articulated jazz piano music,
conceiving myself as on target. I knew my play left
various qualities to be desired; on occasions when
I recorded myself I found the music disjunctive,
rather frantic, and wanting in other respects. I
knew I was not making music like what I heard. But
by virtue of the extent of things I managed at the
piano, the large collection of songs I could play
with command, and what I felt to be an increasingly insider's perspective toward the records I listened to, after a couple of years I regarded myself
as a jazz musician of nearly professional skills. In
some respects the assessment was warranted,
though in others quite pretentious and premature.
I developed many technical skills and a firm working knowledge of the theory of the keyboard, but I
was in some respects as far off the mark as could
be. This was only fully recognized in retrospect, as
shifting manners of play gradually emerged, and
troubles in my prior ways became illuminated,
striking deficiencies in former methods made
transparent by acquisitions much later gained. By
virtue of this lag in my appraisals I was able to sus-

tain motivation to play a good deal without feeling
terribly off-base.

I was learning to play jazz music in what can
be loosely regarded as a backward direction. In
first language learning one initially acquires facility
with a restricted set of terms, and then moves
through an ever more extensive use of capabilities
for new trajectories of movement. I was aimed
from the outset and nearly always in my practicing
for the most complex doings. It was as if one tried
to speak a new language by somehow plunging
right into a serious intellectual conversation, trying
to talk coherently at a proper conversational pace
and, more than that, to deliver a lengthy mono-
logue. This without really knowing how to say any
of the words properly, and without a context of situations and occasions to which the use of the ex-
pressions is affiliated, a give-and-take through
which encouragement to speak and learn to speak
has a practical and interactional import. The pathways allowed this possibility. Having a visual-con-
ceptual means for going places, incorporated into
a tactilely managed set of easeful maneuvers and
the development of varieties of dexterities in
engagement with the terrain, I could at least sustain large streams of conduct at a fast clip from
early into the training. Playing along paths, going
repeatedly through a chord cycle, there was
enough 'jazziness' to my actions that I felt at the
piano I was essentially doing what jazz players do.

Over the course of the first years of my work,
very little playing of this sort was done:

> the book, the book, the book, book, book
> the book, the book, the book, book, book

I was, instead, in pursuit of the most magnilo-
quently organized affairs. Each day the bulk of my
practicing was spent roaming all over the keyboard, rather than lingering in a delimited territory,

mastering certain ways of dealing with a sparsely
textured, small melodic course of movement.

My situation was in fact so highly skewed in a particular direction that it was nearly two years before I began to have an experience with the keyboard that would seem essential to the making of music. It was not until the start of my third year of play that I found myself 'going for the sounds'.

I recall playing one day and finding as I set out into a next course of notes, after a lift-off had occurred, that I was expressly aiming for the sound of those particular notes, that the sounds seemed to creep up into my fingers, that the depression of the keys realized a sound being prepared for on the way down, that I had gone to *do* them, as when walking you bring 'attention' to the sounds of your steps and thereby, by the same token and with that very 'act,' you begin to expressly do the soundedness of your walk. I was not only going for a good place. I was aiming for sounding spots.

Now it was not the case that in my prior play, for two years, I was only going for good places. I was not involved in a game at the keyboard, in some sort of playful preoccupation at developing skill in rapid visual detection, in a test at dexterity management, a crossword puzzle of matching up chord names with run possibilities. I was going for music. I was listening to my records and aiming for that jazz to happen, present and intentionally directed to a course of sounds. It would not have done at all to have played for years on an electric piano with the amplifier turned off. I was filling the room with sounds, sounds having various qualities for me, their qualities in no way distinguishable, however, from the manner in which my filling the room was proceeding.

I knew what the paths sounded like, was not surprised by the sounds of the routes, as one may be startled when accidentally learning on an open keyboard. But what the paths sounded like was known in the way I was making them. There was not one me doing 'listening' and another doing pathway playing. I was listening-in-order-to-make-my-way, in order to find as I played each day that I was doing this jazz music. I recognized the pathways' sounds. They had become quite familiar to me. But it is one thing to recognize familiar sounds you are making and another to be able to aim for particular sounds to happen. A different sort of directionality of purpose and potential for action is involved in each case.

Looking at the matter more closely, what the expression 'going for the sounds' captured for me at the time was the experience of doing a melody. I had been striving for this rapid, fast-flowing, characteristic jazz-sounding course of articulated streams of broad ranging highs and lows. Armed with devices that furnished, of their own accord as it were, a high frequency of jazz 'phonemes,' so that I could hear the jazz-ness of a course through their recurrent articulation, as in mimicking another language the use of some characteristic quality of the sound structure may create a certain resemblance, some 'sounds of jazz' were being done. And more than this, my listening had discovered a range of other qualities. One does not, for example, stay in a given territory or range for too long, but moves up and down the keyboard. One does not go fast and then suddenly break the pace of a melody line, but for reasonable stretches of play maintains a more or less constant rate of articulation. One does not play the same note over and over again, but plays lots of notes. And there were a host of attack and decay qualities. There were rhythmic features of the jazz phrases that I had gradually incorporated into my playing. Jazz, I had long heard, was filled with patterns of slightly shifting metrical forms. It was not a matter only of playing courses of evenly spaced notes—1 1 1 1 1 1 1 1 1 1 1—but some of the most characteristic pacing variations had become almost my stock ap-

proach to particular runs. A long run would, for |
example, often be preceded by a little spate of
three or four notes taken fast—1111 1 1 1 1 1 1 1 1;
the melodic turnaround I referred to above, first
coming down a bit on the diminished scale and
then going all the way up, was characteristically
done with such a metrical structure.

But there was, with respect to the finely textured note-to-note nature of my play, an order that
was guaranteed in the path's formal theoretic construction: for example, alternating half steps and
whole steps. I was not *doing* note-to-note selectional work. I decided where to start out each run,
which run to choose, how fast to play it. But, we
may say, no intentionality of aim was given to particular pitch achievements—only these broad 'par-
ameters' received a motivated determination.

In pursuing the activity we call 'playing a
melody,' satisfaction of the task requires that each
of the definite pitches be achieved. A wrong note
stands out like a sore thumb. While you may simu-
late the melody by passing over the keyboard with
a gesture that vaguely suggests it, by, for example,
going up where it goes up and down where down,
to do the melody correctly is to produce each and
every note, and in proper temporal articulation. In
our musical system and in the jazz I aimed for, it is
successions of particularly pitched, noted affairs
that we attend in encountering what we call the
melody of the music.

I could pick out the melody of a relatively
simple song with no difficulty, but these jazz melodies were complex and fast, and the paths had
furnished a solution to the problems I had encountered.

Playing now, I found myself doing what I
could speak of as 'entering melodically' into the
production, as I began to try to do things that related back to things previously done in ways that
would have been formerly quite impossible. Consider this activity: a course of notes is played dur-

ing the tenure of a particular chord and, when a next chord is played, a course of notes is produced for it that both relates to the new chord and relates 'backwardly' to what has been done before. Such a practice can serve as a useful point of reference for characterizing the essence of this interim stage of my play.

In the earliest pathway playing, what happened on any chord was decided by the choice of an appropriate fitting run *de novo*, each chord at a time. After some while, I began to play a path on a second chord that was formed, relative to this chord, as a first path was related to the first chord. Here is a simple example:

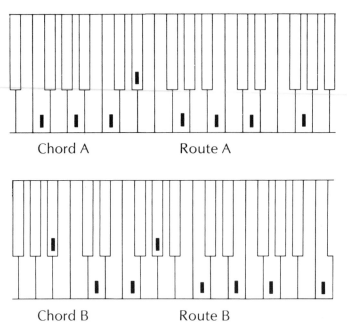

Chord A   Route A

Chord B   Route B

The two melodic lines are similarly constructed, musicologically speaking; each relates to the chord in the same way (a 'major triad' based on the second degree of the chord scale). When a melodic intentionality was instituted, when I began taking up with a course of particular notes as I proceeded, as notes whose particularity of pitch I was aiming

for, much experience had been gained through |
such operations as this, experience that enabled
me to do something congruous with what had been
previously done. At first and for some time this was
a conceptual procedure. I would think: major triad
on second, now again, diminished on third, repeat,
and would do hosts of calculating and guidance
operations of this sort in the course of ongoing
play.

A small sequence of notes was played and
then a next course followed. As the abilities of my
hand developed, in its engagement with the terrain and its own organization as an organ with respect to the terrain, I found myself for the first time
coming into a position to begin to do melodic work
with respect to these courses. I could pick out melodies before, but there was no way, for a long
time, that I could latch on to the details of a pathway course I was doing and then successively do
something with this course of sounds, operate
upon the arrangements of the particular note-to-
note constellations of which it was formed. The
notes of the path seemed to go by too fast for me
to take hold of them; my hand had not developed
that sort of grasp over their working constitution
that permitted taking up with them in ways repetitional melodying involved, in transposing them
accurately, for example. In the third year of play I
began to take hold of the sounds, and note-to-note
selections started to come within hand-full grasp.

The emergence of a melodic intentionality, an
express aiming for the sounds, which in the case of
melody is an aiming for a note-to-note course of
doings, was contingent in my experiences upon the
acquisition of facilities that made it realizable, and
it was not as though in all my prior work I was
trying to do coherent note-to-note melodying and
failing. Motivated so predominantly toward the
rapid course, frustrated in my reproductive hearing
of the recorded piano passages, whatever skills for
melodic construction I had were dormant. The

simplest sorts of melody work entailed a manner of soundful intentionality that had been virtually obliterated as a possibility by the course of my acquisitions.

My new experience with these 'sounds' seemed to illuminate a difficulty among many I formerly had. Compounding the general desperateness of the first-session playing attempts was a most annoying inability to hear myself play. On a small bandstand, with a small spinet, a bass player over one shoulder and drummer the other, I continually felt myself being drowned out, and often played with excessive force to try to hear the piano (complaints I made about the acoustics were ignored, I figured in retrospect, because it looked like a weak excuse for a poor showing).

But it wasn't a matter of not 'concentrating' on the 'sounds,' nor an issue of the loudness of the sounds as they might be measured on an oscilloscope, a deficiency of my 'hearing.' Other players, in fact, seemed to have no trouble in this regard. What was involved in my inability to hear, I reasoned, was that in these earliest sessions there was so little course-ness to the nature of my productions in which, so to speak, I was prospectively and retrospectively involved.

Common experiences can be colloquially cited. A symphony orchestra in an unamplified outdoor amphitheater may sound disappointingly faint from far off in the grass, until one's 'participation' with the unfolding course of the music's melody is engaged, and then the volume seems to increase, so much so that the whole question of 'volume' becomes problematic.

Listening to a conversation at a nearby table, you cannot clearly hear what is being said—it is too remote; but no sooner do you begin to understand a small phrase, to tune in on the details of the talking, than the conversation comes within range.

The experience in melodic doings may inform

former enriches any approach to conceptualizing the latter. Playing a course so that things done are kept alive and brought to pass into and through things currently underway, with a course of gesture that specifically holds on to the detailed interrelationships of the progress—the sounds of melody— is to so proceed that one hears what he is doing, not turning up the volume of the sounds but, from the standpoint of production, undertaking courses of describable bodily activities. To leave the hands out of the 'hearing' enterprise at the piano is to leave music as a production unexamined.

To go for the sounds was now to go for a detailed progression of note-to-note transactions, and to hear the sounds, to have the sounds 'thematically central,' to place the melody as a so-called figure against the background of other sounds of the world, was to be behaving in particular ways. When I look at 'listening' from the standpoint of the producer, when I ask myself 'what is it to go for the sounds?', it is to an inspection of my ways with the keyboard that I turn.

One Saturday morning I thoroughly took my fine grand piano totally out of tune, and spent the most frantic weekend I can remember trying, with the few necessary tools and a manual on *HOW TO TUNE PIANOS*, to put it back into the shape that the tuner accomplished in an hour on Monday morning. The manual described a procedure for tuning that involved a systematic course of adjustments to make by regulating tension on the tuning pin around which the string is wrapped. Two strings are brought into desired alignment by so tightening or loosening one relative to the other that a certain 'wah wah wah wah wah' sound, a pulsation that is apparently perceptible as a result of differing vibration frequencies, is brought to the proper rate. When two notes, say, a 'fourth apart,' from a C to an F, are struck together, there must be a 'beating' of this pulsation of approximately one beat for every two seconds. Two notes are simultaneously struck; one listens to this beat, and adjusts the rate by turning one of the pins with the tuning hammer. Then there is a complex method for proceeding through a cycle of strings, tuning each to the others with elaborate checks along the way (minor errors become terribly cumulative).

I never got past the first page of the manual. I spent nearly all of Saturday hammering away at two notes trying to 'find the beat.' I put my head in between the location of the two strings, figuring that because the beat was a function of some sort of distance between the two, it might be found 'in the middle.' I hit the notes hard, and soft; I tried to listen at the decay end of the sound; I pretended to listen to something else. No beats in sight, let alone one every two seconds.

I later learned that piano tuners spend a course of several months of apprenticeship working with limited pairs of strings, practicing 'hearing the beats.' Their practice consists in developing such a delicacy in the employment of the tuning hammer that a style of movement is acquired that creatively elucidates a beat by ever so slightly varying the tautness of the strings. The piano tuner does not hear beats between pulsating strings by developing a finer 'ear,' and the pulsations are detectably present to an oscilloscope when I strike the keys and when he does (which is to say that the oscilloscope creatively elucidates beats having this quality). He learns by learning how to constitute and ride on the sound waves of a pair of pulsating strings, with his arm and hand artfully engaged with the hammer and pin. I couldn't hear the beat because I so clumsily used the hammer as to never elucidate it through my movements. It was not oscilloscopic sounds the manual talked of in passing; it was the sounds of piano tuning as an arm and hammer enterprise.

As attempting to pay attention, to concentrate, did not bring the sounds of the small spinet

piano into relief in my earliest group play, so
hearing a beat between two sounding notes was
not achieved by focusing my listening, as that is
colloquially and otherwise spoken of. In both
cases, a manner of bodily engagement describes
how 'listening' and 'sounds' are to be described
within the context of the activity at hand.

For the improvisor it is melodying that is done,
and if I engage myself with the sounds of the piano
as the tuner does (which would mean needing a
third arm to move the hammer), I cannot take up
with a course of notes so as to do jazz playing.
Melody sounds are different sounds from the
sounds of vibrating strings, which is to say that
making melodies is a different enterprise than de-
signing pianos, or tuning them, or teaching a
course in physics.

Let's look, then, to what it was that my hands
had been achieving in their ways with the keyboard. I was going for the sounds, for a course of
melody, I began to find that I knew what the next
notes would sound like. But I did not know what a
next note sounded like or where a sounding note lay
on the keyboard, apart from how I was engaged
with this terrain. As I found the next sounds
coming up, as I set out into a course of notes, it
was not as if I had learned about the keyboard so
that looking down I could tell what a regarded note
would sound like. I do not have that skill, nor do
many other musicians. I could tell what a note
would sound like because it was a next sound, because my hand was so engaged with the keyboard
that it was given a setting of sounding places in its
own configurations and potentialities. To describe
these relations, we must look at developments that
had been taking place in my hand's ways with the
keyboard, then return to an explicit discussion of
the meaning of 'going for the sounds.'

Consider first the procedure alluded to above,
executing a course of notes in one chordal context

and then executing a similarly constituted course in a next chordal setting. Musical texts show an 'order' of such repetitions as recurrent features of structure, so conceived and examined. What is it to do a repetition of a figure?

I played a sequence like this on the piano, one that involved going up and then down and turning my hand over the thumb (the numbers below refer to the sequence of the notes and the digits employed: a = thumb, b = second finger, etc.).

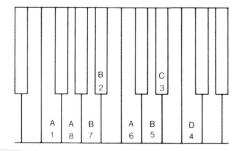

Then I moved to play this figure again with the occurrence of a next chord, and found various possibilities such as:

1. I could play the sequence for the second chord starting on a note relative to that chord as the first is relative to the first. For instance, if the run began on the third tone of the first chord, the new run could be brought to begin on the third tone of the second chord.

2. The new run could have the same internal pitch relationships, but start on a different location with respect to the new chord.

3. The new run could retain the pitch organization of the preceding—the relative place organization, where 'place' here means a place within the theory of half steps and whole steps—but have various alterations with respect to the internal spacing values of the successive tones one to the next, with respect to the intensities, and to tempo.

4. The new run could be in various other ways only 'essentially related' to the preceding run. Say

the first started out slow and went up fast, then doubled back and went fast again, while the second started out slowly and came back down through the same pitches as the first, then doubled back and went fast again, but over different pitches.

There were innumerable variations possible, looking at 'structure' in this way and, corresponding to various continuity practices, ways of the hand were cultivated that were suited to the performance of such maneuvers.

Transposition of such a figure to a new segment and correct repetition with respect to pitch, without an alteration in the pacing structure of the succession, without slowing it down or slowing down parts of it, involved coping with the topography of the terrain by the hand as a negotiative organ with various potentials and limitations.

My hand had ways with the keyboard that allowed repetitions of all sorts to be sustained without error in this sense, but at the same time there were sorts of courses taken whose intact replication, as pitched-spaced sequences, was something I was not equipped to handle. Here is the hand in three different melodic configurations, producing the same intervallically constituted courses:

    To aim for a sequence of reiterated melodic fragments of the above sort required rapidly shifting configurations and realignments for an intervallically 'exact' replication. At the outset of my melodic attempts, exact repetitions, bringing a particularly constituted course to replacement in another sector, corresponding to a next chord, was a common practice of going for the sounds. Here a wrong note stood out like a sore thumb. When a run was produced and an equivalently pitched transposition was quite clearly what the next run started out looking like, where one could tell that the repeat of these particular arrangements was being expressly sought, there was then the possibility

of wrong notes, the sense of whose incorrectness |
was provided by this transactional history.

The keyboard had come under that sort of incorporated control that such operations could be attempted, in the course of ongoing and rapid play, and were attempted with some degree of confidence, but now many mistakes began to occur. Pathway play had become fluent and errorless, an error being a different sort of affair in such ways of proceeding. My beginning melodying, however, was filled with mistakes, their status and nature given by the procedure that grabbed for an exactly pitched-spaced repetition.

A rapid and intricately winding passage would be played and then its reiterated production in an upcoming chordal context sought, doing melodying in this mode, and while many such attempts would come close, a good number fell enough off the mark, constraining myself as I did this way, that a distinct sense of struggling to make it happen now marked such improvisational work. I began to sound like someone trying hard to say something.

In this setting of movable parts so easily having a voice of their own with only the slightest slips of the hand, I made quite sophisticated lungings for melody, aiming for highfalutin sayings particularly said. Rather jazz-like strips would be played, now asking for longevity.

As I reached for one of them, I knew more or less where it lay. Distancing capabilities had developed such that I was able to move up to a good next position for a reiteration. And pathway playing had made the terrain available as a setting of places known in terms of the shifting course of chords. As I played a chord and then a next one, the new chord furnished a sector of engagement, established a dimensionalized range of axes, in which the hand going for a saying could locate itself, and between the chordal hand's pose and the melodic hand's stretch for reiterative action, there was no longer a strict relationship of 'theoretic correctness.' Reiterations would not necessarily occur in precisely similar locales, a first course relative to its chord as a second was then to be to its.

I would get to a good next place to begin a reiterative run, and at first go for its exactly pitched replication there. With a class of courses there was 'no trouble.' With others there were mistakes made. I was often very close to where a correct repeat would be, but at a rapid tempo there was no time for checking out matters, and I would try to make the restatement happen even while making mistakes, so that a mistake would stand out as an error in the very attempt at least to get the rest of it right. There was an ambitiousness of the aim unmindful of the difficulties, a reliance upon locational facilities and configurational shifts that would suffice for doing much of the replication, but an imprudence at the same time with respect to details of the newly contoured locale with which the intended passage would have to cope.

The hand was able to get into a good next arena, to find harmonically consonant nodes for arrival and orientation along the way, established by tonicities in an acquired togetherness of the chordal-melodic engagement, and much of the replication was successfully accomplished. Shifting lumps on the surface were well under a general mobile and repositional control, but the demands of the fragment to be reiterated, going for a duplication this way, met resistance in the effort to sustain adherence to its intact paced preservation, with a never-changing tempo.

The hand came into the new territory for a repetition, found a con-chordant location for its sensible statement, found that the doing could be well done there, and it came down into the sector ready to play there. Putting down there, what being there now would be like, what there would be as a setting for the hand, for its axial relationship to the topography there, it came in as a hand only partially in trouble.

Moving up to a locale, the breadth of the place being aimed toward, its extensiveness or compactness, the edges to be contended with there, the layout of highs and lows, these had been placed and sustained in operational scale by a hand that had its bearing. It was a hand that had a bearing with respect to the contours, and their respective distances, for in its very constitution as a hand at home in the keyboard, what *keys* were like anywhere was appreciated. High off the keyboard, the presence of a field of keys, to be engaged by a spread and arched, pointed configuration, lay beneath the fingers. It was a field of keys whose stability and horizontality relative to the body was assured in the hand's relationship to the arm's and shoulder's angularities. It was a field of keys whose strict, rather than encircling, horizontality was found by arms and hands that extended outwardly from the body's center, at the same time as they managed a proportionally proper extension away from the trunk. It was a field of keys whose dimensions throughout were stable, so that extensions required of the hand that, however it was spaced over some scope, a precisely corresponding relative spatial configuration had to be sustained through extensions and contractions of the arms' lateral movements. They moved far off to a side, while the hands retained *that* keyboard as its field for engagement.

In an appraisal of the space, a bearing is taken by the thumb, as in this photograph:

Appraising the crack between two keys, as a crack
occupying so much space against that thumb, ap-
preciating the magnitude of the crack as a breadth
of contact along the thumb's surface, a presence is
thereby gained to the size of things at hand
throughout the domain of actual or hovering hold
over the territory as an extending field. And more
than this: a thumb capable of participating in a rescaling for the hand as each of 'its parts' can do for
the rest should the crack be somewhat tighter, as in
the small-scaled setting of a child's toy piano,
which in a moment of adjustment becomes a
familiar keyboard again to hands with essentializing ways of knowing how to be at home in an exploratory setting of keys.

Striving so intently to make a saying happen,
there was frequently this sort of a way: I would go
for some reiteration by lunging for general shapes
and ordering of a prior figure. The first course had
a particular intervallic construction, there were
highs and lows within the sweep of the gesture,
and a manner of pacing. An extension would on
occasions aim not so much for the achievement of
these particularly spaced arrays of highs and lows,
for a precise pitch duplication in terms of
whole-step distances. But I moved forward instead
for a course that went more or less high where the
first went high, low where the first had been low, a
course of meander that retained various essential
nodes of the fragment. And a hand had been
fashioned that could come down into the chordally
implicated sector and get itself into *particular
notes* so as to realize these essential similarities, to
bring a generalized sequential shaping into a particular keyed expression. It had become a hand
knowing how to enter into a scope of the field, and
do a line of shaped movement through the course
as a course of particular keys. There had been developing, through extensive pathway maneuvering,
a hand having ways of notefully being in a sensible
scope, and not always, in this phase, with a strictly

duplicating aim. I began building continuities whose melodicality was an essentialization of what could be characterized as precedingly accomplished sayings. And I became able to gradually do such work because my hand could find, through the ways of its entrance into a sector, keys-at-hand there.

Keys were at hand in a sector for me in ways that displayed my hand's growing improvisationality in its overall approach to terrain engagements. The classical artist operates under the constraints of a score to be articulated and intoned in a particular manner. He operates within a social organization of professional certification, excellence, and competitiveness differing from that which I was in, as a jazz aspirant, his circumstances placing extraordinary demands upon a faithfulness to the score, where what 'faithfulness' and 'the score' mean is defined by that social organization.

For jazz, it was more an in-course note-to-note selection as a sustained line of action toward which I aimed, and having the hand touch the surface with a broad and palmed appraisal, for example—not now as a means of groping for particular 'notes' as a beginner with closed eyes might employ such a contact—was to have a way of securing 'sorts of places' in which 'sorts of action' could be taken.

A broadly palmed appraisal may be part of a handful appreciation of a territory for variously shaped maneuvers (which would have to proceed through particular keys to be sure). And this extended, sector-surveying hand here not only finds 'keys,' placements and distances of particularly depressable spots, but contours of the territory whose relevance fits now within the conduct of classes of gestural maneuvers.

Consider how the extended fingers might appreciate the two-ness-three-ness of the black notes. Such 'gestalting tactilities,' topographic-distancing appraisals, had been developing all along, for conduct of all sorts—from playing a scale to finding a next location in an arpeggio—involved their use from my earliest days of keyboard experience. But as continuities were now being expressly sought, and as the hand moved for sequences of action essentially implicated by a preceding figure, abilities with the two-ness-three-ness aspect of the terrain figured into newly organized courses of action.

The hand would appraise the two-ness-three-ness layout in order to find, for example, how much space was available for doing noted-work in a sector, how that sort of cross-over pivoting required to be essentially true to a foregoing remark could be managed with respect to the available space at hand in a new locale, and under such motivations the very sense of an assessed extent of space, of what the mounds were, had undergone transformation.

More was now beginning to be appreciated than the number of particular notes for particular fingers, more than an opening filled with this or that in particular, more than a grasping of where some named note was. Under melodic guidance toward the essential reiteration of a prior gestural course, the hand needed to find in an 'amount of space': that there was the kind of room to be moved about in to carry out a desired course; that a space being grasped was that 'sort of space' into

which a thumb could be brought, so that you could
get up higher by getting a thumb down 'around
there'; that sort of space beyond which might be a
path to fall back upon; that sort of space to be
avoided were I only going slow enough to avoid it;
that sort of space where somewhere therein is
probably a usable note. The two-ness-three-ness
appraisal had differing significances within these
classes of actions, and in much of my melodying
efforts there was, attached to the appreciation of
the good things I was finding to do beneath the
hand, the discovery of a stretch of rapids coming
up, as it were, too fast.

A mistake now turned out to be a different sort
of matter. As shapes of sequential movement became ways of melodying, wrong notes were here
not given that sort of relief and sense they received
in the context of clearly failing duplications. At
times now, almost inadvertently, the hand unable
for many courses to pay off on its immediate history with an intervallically precise restatement, the
very work of doing a replication now became only
one means to melody, and a new practice was
being added to the hand's repertoire of ways. There
was, then, not only a taking up of something done
before, and replacement in its pitched specificity
at an upcoming sector, but a way of entering the
topography with both key places and arenas for
improvisational action accessibly there. A hand
was developing that was possessed of mobile ways
with the topography, ways permitting the attempt,
at least, to make the best of things.

But there was at this phase of my studies still a
struggle for melody to be expressly done, an adherence to chord-specific prior shapes, and as the
hand moved to a then specifically next sector,
shapes were *given* an historical integrity (and the
complexity of continuity practices increased), with
a working to make it happen. There was more of
this, here, than that sort of making-the-best-of-
things to only later emerge, a way of being with the

keyboard that would be continuously prudent rather than struggling to get about sensibly. Here I was very much backward looking and reparatively forward going.

I would set out into a new territory for a next chord, do a gesture that replicated the prior sequentially intricate move, and find that I could preserve some of its features, sometimes exactly, sometimes glossingly. And at times I would find that a bit of this got done in the next chordal context and there would still remain a period of tenure for the chord's duration to be filled up with melody. The hand finished the parts of the preceding that it could melodically manage, some of whose sounds it could pre-hear on the way down because there was an assured note target for its aim in the new sector. The hand then had—this fast jazzy player I was always trying to be—more to do. Not playing seemed to make the music stop.

As the hand did the things it was seeking to do 'singingly,' it had at the same time been becoming a hand able to do all sorts of things everywhere. I would play a figure, go for its repetition, get some way into it, and stumble. To fill what I felt to be the remaining empty space, keeping this jazz going, I would do something quite unrelated to the explicit continuities I had partially achieved. I would accomplish the beginning of a reiteration (transposition, inversion, pitched-essential duplication, exact duplication, etc.), and then, for example, use up a remaining alloted chord-time by taking on any notes that were thereabout to take.

There were the familiar pathways, and these could at times be got onto, but, with respect to the integrity of the sought continuity of the statement, they were 'any notes thereabout' that would keep the action underway. Not quite that, however, for they were filled with their characteristic jazz sounds. The originally sought replication had its characteristic jazz sounds here and there within it. And there was a melodying being done with them,

aimed-for continuities so that the strips were being |
brought together into statements of a sort. There
was, as well, an organization of particularly
pitched chordal sounds, and these other charac-
teristic-sounding little afterthoughts stuck on the
end of an increasingly coherent linkup. From a
virtual hodgepodge of 'phonemes' and approximate
'paralinguistics,' there was a 'sentential structure'
slowly taking shape, sayings now being attempted,
themes starting to achieve cogent management.
But at the same time, courses of action were being
sustained that faded and disintegrated into stam-
merings and stutterings, with 'connectives' only
later to become integrally part of the negotiative
proceedings.

These any notes thereabout were not only the
places on pathways that I attempted to stick at the
end of a gesturally guided continuity, for there had
developed ways of moving around courses that
could not, by this point, be any longer described in
terms of a path's traverse. There is the chromatic
scale in its theoretical organization, every note on
the keyboard going up and down. It may be played
in strict orderly progression, expressly as a chromatic run. But then there was a way of proceeding
that had been gained through manipulations along
it and paths like it, a way that could be called a
chromatic *way* of going about.

Take the index finger and the fourth finger,
the fingers touching two black notes, the hand in
that sort of configurational posture adopted when
being chromatically situated and engaged. An index and fourth finger touch two closely spaced
black keys, in a chromatic way of being. The keyboard is a setting of places, with measurable dimensions. The hand is an 'organ' with measurable
dimensions. The knowing relationships obtaining
between them, the way the hand finds itself correspondingly configurated to fit dimensions of this
keyboard, involves a mobile hand engaged in a
course of action.

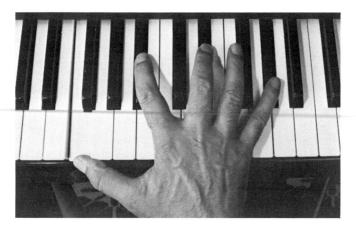

When the hand is broadly arrayed as here, the distances required to move about between the second
and fourth fingers may be known because a *sort* of
course is being taken. There is a globalized appreciation for the fourth-ness of a course (as a possibility in this photo), or a 'chromaticality,' and the
hand did not always come into the keyboard for a
first note and then a second note particularly, but
would, as well, enter the terrain to take a certain
essential sort of stride. The distance between the
second and fourth fingers in the spread configurations may be given its determination by the assumption of a stance for a *style* of keyboard engagement, in which the shaping of the digits'

spread is not unrelated to the way the entire hand
is shaped for such a course.

Two years of pathway manipulations taught me a 'chromatic way' of engaging with the terrain, and coming into this chromatic way, the hand assumed a posture, the fingers bunched up into a preparatory shape, and where notes along the chromatic path lay was thereby anticipated in the hand's posturing for a sector to be chromatically taken. The second finger finds a place relative to the fourth and the fourth relative to the second, as they find themselves together spaced within a hand chromatically configurating.

In the 'chromatic way' my hand could be aimed toward any sector in sufficiently prepared shape, precisions then to be 'toned up' as the contact was made. As one finger in this chromatically poised hand makes contact, it finds where in the depth and width of the key it is, and the hand's chromaticality becomes correspondingly toned for the sector's dimensions running off in both directions from the point of appraised contact.

Such a chromatic way involved a stance where the thumb stayed back, away from the black notes, and with that alignment a course could be taken regardless of where the starting point of a setdown happened to be. A host of ways of generally entering into the terrain were gained, postural modalities acquired; and when specifically sought, soundful melodying got into trouble, it was in the availability of such ways that any notes thereabout could be errorlessly handled on occasion, say when a reiterative attempt ended with time 'left over' to be filled with keyboard activities.

To call it a 'chromatic way' is more than this, for it was not only that a globalized shaping potential had been gained, but a new way of moving along the 'chromatic path' itself emerged, and became a prominently used resource in my playing at this point. I would come down chromatically, and then play a course of notes that was only 'essentially chromatic,' not following the strict path that prescribes every adjacent key, but one that had that sort of bunchedness to it. A course followed not each and every note on the chromatic scale, but had a generalized 'chromaticality,' with, for example, whole steps interspersed within a 'correct' chromatic passage, so that this way would pass over a set of places like this.

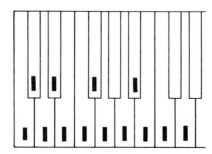

There were a host of such ways of being that had developed, generalized ways, ways done everywhere, ways gained from pathway playing but now freed from the routes on whose traverse the ways were first acquired, freed by a striving toward melodicality. There were scaling ways, and up-a-little-down-a-little ways, rocking ways, and every-other-finger ways, and skipping ways, hopping ways, rippling ways, ways to go a long way with, and more.

In the availability of such ways as shaped means of approach, and their use as generalized modes of transaction, were afforded potentials for keeping action going in a sector, for making streams of notes, for doing a fair amount of unthoughtful, weakly geared aimings for sounds. They allowed sustaining, at the same time, a connective tissue of action within attempts to tie up courses taken with one chord to those taken with the next, and for maneuvering about in styles that would, over the course of my next year of studies, come to figure most prominently into what making the best of things continuously would require.

In this phase of play I was 'going for the sounds' with an altogether unsteady consistency. If the note beneath the thumb is engaged (a B), what that note beneath the first finger will sound like (an Eb) may be known:

It is known in that not only was the finger aimed to a place, but the singing me was directed to a destination. It was known not as a sounding-vibrating-string's-lever, but as a place in a course of unfolding and struggling encounters with the terrain. This sense of 'knowing what it would sound like' can be suggested.

You sing a sequence of notes. There is a pitch-edness here. Exaggerating the production's expressiveness, the head and torso and inner structures of the mouth quite noticeably rise and fall. That is what doing a pitched course of movements is about. In a little 'experiment' undertaken as I reflected upon this knowing of the sounds, I found that if several tones are sung, a two or three noded passage made, while facing a mirror, the successive pitches of the notes involve an up and down movement of the head in fairly precise correspondence. Watching where I was aligned, marking the opening position of my nose vis-à-vis the mirror with a chalk, as I passed through several sung steps, chalking the location of my head at the arrival vicinity of each, the vertical array of resultant chalkmarks corresponded to the arrangement of pitches (relatively speaking) that a score would graphically freeze.

There is a concordant system of pitched-shaped movements grossly and only suggestively portrayed at this level, between, simplying matters, the vertical movements of the head and the horizontal spread of the fingers on the terrain. To go for the sound, to find what a next sound will be like, is to be somehow synchronously directed along these various dimensions. The thematic presence of a melodic course, of sounds, is given in a sustained togetherness of such aiming at the keyboard.

But it is intricate indeed, for we have not precise relativities here, as though we satisfy, in our destinational structures of movement, requirements of a strictly scaled graph. The contours of a sung progression can outline its shapes with a minuscule and miniaturized line of action, while the synchronously linked, aimfully partnered hand moves across a fixed-sized grid. And more than this, there can be an absence of any sense of motion in the mouth and its parts, the rising and falling pitches that a singing entails may be transferred into a head movement that laterally proceeds, as if the very head and shoulder were doing 'high' and 'low' in moving sideways. The coupling of aim—the sort of coordinational, axial, essentializing, rescaling, gestural compressing, transferring capabilities— of which a synchronously aimed body is in possession, was variously refined and ragged in this stage of my improvisational play.

It is not simply that being with the thumb on this B I knew that the Eb was the place to melodically go. In a reiterative attempt such an interval had been previously played, and now I went for that distance again. In a new mini-land-

these two fingers were part of a hand that established its overall shape, by, for example, the other
fingers' appraisal of my general location within a
keyboard setting where this particular desired interval would particularly be. The pinkie (see the
above photograph) may anchor a scope of spread,
feeling an open space, finding the significance of
this open space by reference as well to the fourth
finger's appreciation of the outer edge of those
three black-note mounds. The feel of how much
key is under the extended finger aids likewise in the
hand's appraisal of the Eb's place, not only along
the horizontal axis, but as a place whose depth and
dimensions are present as well.

For many actions such appraisals may not be
necessary, however, and indeed only in the beginner's hand must contact be regularly made to aid in
place finding. But when shifts of ranges occur,
when a broad leap is taken, the slightest contact
may help tone up the places.

Now, when it was a matter of not only finding
a particular, single intervallic transposition, the repetition of a 'third' for example, as with these two
fingers, but one of winding with the hand into a
new arena for melody, where the negotiative transactions entailed more than keeping the scale and
its contours in tactile regard, then possibilities
arose for various imprecisions in the togetherness
of the gesture.

In this phase of play, I would go for a reiteration, beginning with such an interval as this 'pair,'
its location assuredly sought and known, pre-hear-
ing its forthcomingness in that fact. But with respect to the continuing course I would find a
pitched-spaced preservation not manageable, in
the ways I went about it. An essential shaping of
the gesture (highs where high, lows where low,
same number of notes, a bunch of notes that appears as dense, similar relative pitchedness) could
perhaps be brought off reasonably well. But forth-

coming notes, after the opening, were not particular sounding spots in the way the synchronously sung and assuredly targeted opening was a particular sounding spot. And instead of really knowing what the next notes would sound like, I would be saying some of them particularly and definitely and others would be, as it were, speaking back to me. Doing melodying, going for particularly pitched transactions, in this phase of play thus had a characteristic unevenness, 'me' trying to have the hands say this in particular, the hands saying some of what I took them to say but not everything, and then saying things of their own rather inappropriate choosing.

A recurrent piece of advice had been given in the jazz subculture when discussions were had of ways to develop skills at improvisation: sing while you are playing. In pathway playing I was singing what I played only after the fact, and actually felt foolish trying to follow the advice. It was like trying to keep up with what another says as he is talking along. Now I was intermittently playing what I was singing, but my singing had something of a life of its own. Sometimes its aims were realized, often only their essential shapes brought to fruition, and at other times a greater discrepancy arose out of a lack of synchronicity between movements toward good next sounds that 'I' would project and movements the hands had to be doing in going toward good next places.

It was as if the enterprise of melodying too often came under the jurisdiction of an artful listener, and had I been able to jump into the keyboard with my tongue, matters would have been smoothed out. There had by now developed a 'capacity' for melodying in jazz ways, through my listening and increasing refinement of what these characteristic jazz sounds were like. It was not simply that more practice at getting complex scale-shifting skills was what I needed (though more practice would be had). It was, instead, that there had yet to develop ways of doing melodying where the sorts of well-intentioned reachings that were now getting me into trouble would be replaced by other means of traverse.

The problem of knowing what the sounds will sound like, central for all improvisors, requires more detailed explication. If I strike a first note and then reach for a second, I may not know what it will sound like. I may find, in either manifest or minute bodily movements 'accompanying' the finger's journey, that I vocally appreciate a vicinity of places into which the finger will settle.

If I am played a note on the keyboard and then asked to sing another note nearby that is pointed to, I can generally do so, but usually only by singing some orderly path that links together the notes and whose steps I may count until I reach the indicated target on which it lies (say, a major scale). I do not have perfect pitch generally, or any specialized version of perfect pitch that would enable me to make such visual tone identifications.

Although the 'vicinity' of a second note is appreciated as a vague target of the body's move, there is, in a weekly geared aiming, a generalized imprecision of presence with respect to much of the sounding territory.

The sound from 1 to 2 in the diagram

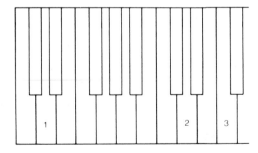

is not aimfully appreciated, as a stretch of generalized vocal movement, to be below that from 1 to 3. It is by assuming an arbitrary stance at 2 that I find 3 to be higher, in an imagined reach for these places when they are pointed at. When in the course of play in a sector they are even slightly out of reach, 2 and 3 may lie 'up there' more or less undifferentiated.

Playing a blues, I began, for example, with a course of notes that can be shown as follows:

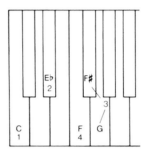

(The '3' notes, an F# and G, are virtually struck together; see below.)

The choice of the opening pair of notes was made 'by reference to' the blues scale, an intervallic construction that always 'works' in the context of the blues, and I went for the C and Eb, taking my bearing there on the sector, with that scale furnishing an initial postural approach to the keyboard. I did not explicitly aim for the sound of the C, that is, move toward it from the outset as an integrated and melodically targeted move. When it was articulated I was immediately grounded, however, and the Eb was a place toward which I was then concertedly directed.

I moved toward the Eb's place concertedly because the blues was being played. I was aligned from the outset toward a bluesy encounter, and the 'minor third interval' realized a paralinguistic component of the posture being initially activated. Setting out to play a blues, if I played a D instead of an Eb for some reason, it would indeed surprise me. So the second note, the Eb, was soundfully given not because I knew the distance of a minor third especially well (though I know that distance in the context of a guessing-game situation), and in

fact by statistical reasoning a D, the second note |
on the major scale, probably my most ancient acquisition, would have had a 'high' expected cer-
tainty with respect to its sound. The soundedness
of the note was given because I was playing the
blues.

The question of the known-ness of the F#, the
third note, cannot be treated apart from the
known-ness of the G. The movement here was not
so much toward 'two notes' as it was toward a characteristic jazz sound, and the F# was articulated in
the course of a move that almost brings the two
fingers into sounding contact at the same time.
(Notated as a 'grace note,' in jazz it is given less
distinctness than such figures are accorded in
much of the classical repertoire where, while not
sustained independently enough to warrant full-
fledged size on the staff, they are articulated as
two clearly separable tones.) On the piano, the
movement that brings the fingers to a pair of keys,
in a blues context of this sort, is almost a striving
toward an in-between tone that the voice or saxo-
phone can achieve. Operating in a blues context, I
assumed a tight little 'nasal' shaping in the course
of the hand's movements away from the Eb, and
adopting a blues stance, this little nasal interdigitation was part of an overall bodily posture that had,
as it were, nasality arrayed all over it.

If I play a C and Eb and move to an F# and rest
there, the F# that I 'hear' appears markedly flat
when I juxtapose this action with the production of
the figure in the above example. Even slowing it
down, when the F# is followed directly by a G, it
appears in my 'hearing' to be distinctly higher than
an F# stably landed upon.

From the standpoint of my aim toward the
sounding place, such differences in 'contextual
soundedness' must be conceived in terms of the
sort of course aiming that I was doing. When I
went for the F# in the context of a bluesy articulation, I did not go for the F# whose qualities could

be isolated from my manner of going. I did not aim for *the* sound, in fact, and in the linkage that was established in my concerted aiming, in my knowing where I was going, was an integrated reaching for a sounding place within an organized course of action.

As I went for the F#, I went for a place-bluesily-on-the-way-to-a-very-nearby-place. Standing outside the perspective of the ongoing accomplishment, an F# so located appears sharper than an F# landed upon. Within the course of my soundful aimings, this sharpness of one F# and flatness of another must be conceived in terms of courses of aimfully targeted and shaped movements, and contexts of such movements. An F#-taken-in-passing, of the above sort, leans upwardly into the note above it, and when I went for this sound I was going for *that* sort of an F#. The one rested upon has its qualities similarly given and appreciated in the fact of the rest. Within the course of play, 'what I was hearing,' and what I was aiming for in 'aiming for sounds'—such matters receive finer formulation below.

To know the sound of the F at which the phrase came to rest was to be aimed toward a place in terms of the organization of the preceding notes. I aimed for a sounding F, and went down into the F knowing where I was going. How was this knowledge organized?

It was not the case that I knew what the F would sound like because I know what F's sound like. Nor was it that I knew what the F would sound like because I had played a G, that I took my bearing on the G and knew what a note 'one whole step below' would sound like. Nor, still, was it by virtue of having played a note a 'whole step' below the F (the Eb), and then one 'whole step' above the F (the G), that I had narrowed in on what a sound 'in between' would sound like. I knew what the F would sound like because the F was part of a 'blues scale' way of handfully being in the terrain. Complexities here require attention.

When I say I know what a note will sound like, I mean that I am engaged in a *course that provides for that note's sound*, that I have a way of moving to the upcoming notes in such a fashion that the handful context of moving to them makes them upcoming notes that will have known sounds. I do not know a note's sound apart from the context of a handful course in which its sound will figure, not now or in this earlier phase of play.

I would, for example, make a statement and go for an exact repetition, and there would be notes in addition to the ones I had played that *could* be soundfully gone toward, if I could manage to do new notes in the transformation while going fast. If I played a figure like this, to take a very simple example:

Bb dominant chord   C major run

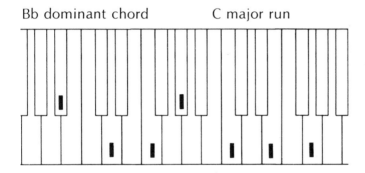

and then went for its replication on a new chord and a new place with respect to that chord:

Eb dominant chord   F major run

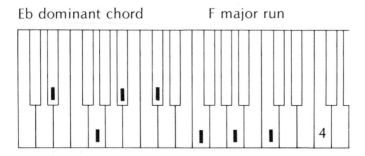

it is not the case that the fourth note above, for example, would not be soundfully approachable.

The major triad here establishes a territory of related sounds. If I play a major triad I can aimfully go for the 'octave,' as in the case of this fourth note, and I know what it will sound like. This is not because of some intrinsic relationships that obtain in the nature of the tones' acoustic construction, but because I have learned a soundful way of moving around the configurational structures of a major triad. Its tones are soundfully given to me because, for example, I do arpeggios through many ranges of the keyboard with this chord, because the known-ness of the distance to get to any of the notes in the triad, no matter in what inversion it is played, has become established as a 'system' of essentialized distance achievements through various manners of configuration.

It is an 'essentialized distance achievement' in, for example, the following senses. I can play a major triad's notes (here shown in simultaneously depressed position for the sake of illustration), with these fingers:

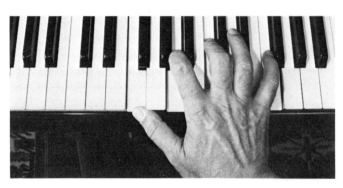

And the distance from the C (the third depressed key from the left) to the higher F (the octave note beneath the little finger) can be securely traversed. I do not know 'distances between keys' in general, I know them in a context, always, of unfolding courses. I know them within arenas of essential hand distancing, and with a configurational facility. This is established through extensive work with ordered constellations of places. I do not know the distance from this C to the F, in this photo:

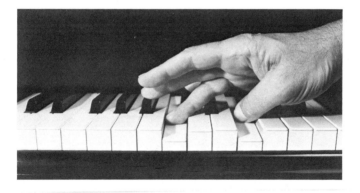

because I know how to move up 'fourths' with that sort of turn-under arrangement. In fact it is an 'awkward' maneuver, so to speak. But, in the context of the hand finding itself anywhere engaged in an F major triad, such turn-unders can be at least securely targeted. This is because, relative to a configurational shaping with which the C (above) is passed through, from among the repertoire of 'ways to be through this place within particular courses,' *that* triad is part of a presence at the keyboard: the F major triad course within which the C has been enunciated, and through which the C can be used as a launching pad.

The distance from the C to the F, in the case of the above examples, is not known because my fourth and little fingers know how to span such a distance, nor because my third and little fingers know it as well. While these fingers are at home with such spreads, they are fingers shaping within a hand that is engaged not simply with distances between notes but with distances in a *way-full context of ordered arrangements*. The reach from the C to the F, done with the various 'digits,' is informed by the stance and course being taken through the hand, and it is by reference to this course at hand that such distances are appreciated and achieved.

With the middle finger on the C, the amount of spread required for the little finger to reach the F is assessed by reference to the ways the other 'fingers' are engaged and by, as well, the way the unused fourth finger informs the shaping of the hand, in this constellation for example:

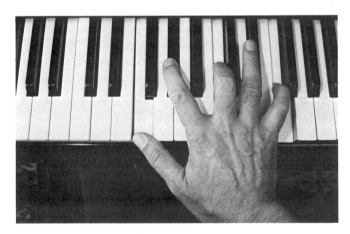

The reach necessary to get to F here is not unrelated to how the second finger finds itself situated, the axial position of the right side of the hand quite

different in this minor triad configuration. Where |
the F lies relative to the C becomes, then, more
than simply a distance along a strictly linear and
horizontal scale. In ongoing play, aiming for a next
sound within a course, one must get to where a
note lies so as to depress it, and depress it without
striking neighboring tones, and while going on and
coming from other places. And how high the rest
of the hand is, the contours the hand as a whole assumes, and the shaping of distances running along
every dimension are of critical importance.

In the course of doing a major triad, to say
that I know where notes of the major triad definitely are, to say that I can be aimed to them synchronously, is to say that I have a secure way of
going to them, and going to them so as to play
them. *From the standpoint of play, the very
soundedness of the note is part of the security of
an aim toward a definite place in the context of a
course of essentially traversable places.* If I project
a sung sound, going upwardly, and bring a finger-
within-the-routing-hand toward that destination, I
find a placeful realization of my aim as a concerted
accomplishment. But by the same token, it is not
the case, as we shall eventually see, that in doing
jazz improvisation I project a sung sound independent of how the hand finds itself situated. I move
instead through courses that provide for definite
soundful theres, that are present for the hand as
ways with which essentialized traversing capabilities have been firmly acquired.

But in this phase of my play, I would often go
for a next place that was not targetable within the
realm of the hand firmly situated in such courses,
and which, in consequence, was therefore a key
and not a sounding place from the standpoint of
my aim. The move toward melody to be made
would involve me in reaching for places indefi-
nitely, which is not to say that I could not bring the
fingers to particular keys (for that had become a
generalized capability of my hands' ways). It is to

say that I was not taking my fingers to places implicated by the context of a handful course of an
exploration providing for other possibilities securely about and sought. And when I say that I
would go for some of the sounds, this is to say that
at times I was going for notes in ways that would
provide for their soundfulness. This is because
definitely targeted moves were handfully implicated by preceding and forthcoming essentialized
configurations.

To go for a sound is to go for a sound within a
course. From the standpoint of the production of
sounding courses, it is in terms of securely targeted movements, implicated by preceding-forth-
coming-positional-configurations, that the definition of sound is to be sought in the first place.
Whatever relevance to the production those 'happenings' in the 'air space' may have (one version of
which is provided in an oscilloscopic creation), we
must explore their relevance, and description as
'real worldly sounds,' within a bodily system of essentially organized movements and distancing
configurations. It is from such a perspective that a
theory of 'listening' might be developed, that the
work of an 'ear' in such a 'system' might be productionally conceived.*

If I play some notes on the major triad, I know
what others on the triad sound like. That is, I know
how to get to a place soundfully. But not always. It

*A relevance of these happenings can be initially sug-
gested. My securely targeted moves toward next sounding
places, as an integrated achievement, requires that I 'hear'
such sounds with my 'ears,' subject to variations I elaborate
below (see the footnote on p. 149) in order to 'tone up' the
precisions of my synchronous aims. Playing an electric piano,
the amplifier bypassed, its sounds recorded on the tape recorder, unable to hear the sounds in the room, singing while I
play, standing outside the perspective of production and
'comparing the pitches' of my singings and fingerings, I find:
precisions of pitch coincidence to be integrated through the
body via these real-worldly-happenings-to-be-'eared.' Discrepancies between 'specific pitch achievements' can be
found when the 'ear' does not participate in these aimings.

is not simply playing notes that 'happen to lie' on
the triad which delineates clearly implicated distance traversals, targetable moves that can be destined to places, thereby accorded soundingness. I
must be 'major-triadly-engaged' with the notes of
the major triad for its sounding places to lead me
to others. In the context of some other manipulation, along other sorts of routes that the hand has
learned to essentially traverse, the 'tones of the
major triad' are not of a major triad *way* of keyboard engagement. From the standpoint of play,
the 'major triad' is not a collection of isolatable
notes with their sounds. It is an arena at hand for
configurationally distanced maneuvers.

To be major-triadly-engaged is not to necessarily play all the notes of a major triad. I would at
this phase of my studies play a figure like the
following:

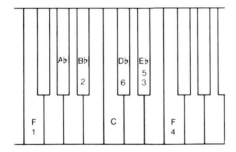

and the Db, the sixth note, would not be soundfully approached. It would be produced as among
the any notes thereabout, tagged on so as to fill out
the 'remaining time.' I would be involved in a
course of maneuvers that did not provide for that
space having soundfulness. Consider ways in
which its soundfulness could be provided. There
are at least a very large number of possible courses
in which its presence as a 'secure there' can be
handfully had.

For it to be securely there is not only to say
that I can move to the first black note of a 'twosome' from the second, that I can go from an Eb to

a Db, that I can bring my finger squarely down into the center of the note without slipping. It is securely there as a place on a *course* within which it occurs.

It may be within a course in the following way. Going down from an Eb to a Db I may be Ab-majorly-engaged with the terrain. And the Db occupies a potential position within an Ab-major-way. I was proceeding through a course that did not have this place, for example, prospectively on it. This is not to be seen by reference to the theoretic relationships obtaining in the preceding notes. Indeed, all the preceding tones lie on an Ab major *scale*. The prospectivity of the Db, as a place on the path, is determined by the way the path is being traversed. This 'way' must be preliminarily clarified.

As the hand was going up the preceding course of notes, it was not proceeding up them in those ways that an Ab-major-way entails. These ways are of a very large class, for a maneuverability around axes of major scale paths greatly compounds the potential essentializing complexities, relative to the 'triad' example given above. As in that example, so in a major scale way, it can be approached from all sides, coming down or up, from the middle outwardly, with many fingering possibilities, taken either sequentially or in various step-skipping ways, played by moving from its ends toward the middle with a rocking-in, and many more. Through all such variations, the hand has *that* course thematic to it, in having deeply essentialized grasp of its presence as a course of definite theres at hand.

In the case of this example, the Db was an afterthought, in that its production was not embedded in some way or class of ways of an Ab-ness character. And, moreover, not only was the Ab-major-way not in some manner part of the way of the journey, neither was any other sound-giving course with this place in its domain (and there are

many other 'paths' that would similarly provide for |
its sound, say a diminished scale).

For a sound-giving course with this Db place in its domain to be operative, it need not be the case that notes on the sound-giving course were formerly played *as* notes on that *particular* sound-giving course. The Db could have been enunciated as the beginning of an Ab way into which the hand was moving as it moved from the Eb. In that case, the Db's soundedness would have been retrospectively established by the forthcoming ways in which it would figure.

It isn't that it would be retrospectively 'sounded.' For in the way it would be taken, in such a 'path-switching' action, it would have been a Db whose sound was given as a definiteness of handful aim, as a launching toward a new path. Its being definitely there, and thus having targetable sound, is being there on the way toward the course it initiates. The definiteness of aim is never merely a secure aim toward *a* place. The gesture's surety is given in the movement toward a key and at the same time through a key, and when a key is entered without its future and past wheres securely present in the unfoldingly routing hand, the hand encounters the terrain other than when it's struck on the way to and from other definite wheres.

The sound-there-routing hand is one that finds places with a definiteness of aim toned up by a shaping for the course within which an articulation occurs. As the Db is being gone toward, from the Eb on the way to a C, Bb, and Ab, for example (tones that lie on an Ab way), *where* the Db really *is*, for a hand going to it, is defined by the shaped course that will bring the finger into the note.

The finger taking a Db in such a downward Ab way is a finger taking *that* Db to be followed by a thumb, and a crossover rotation, and the prospective orientations of the hand toward these forthcoming maneuvers tones up a definiteness of a particular sort of Db landing. The way a finger so comes into a key is an intrinsic part of how we must speak of 'where that key is.' There is no place that can be called the Db place. There are, productionally speaking, Db's for the hand to achieve wayfully. The self-same locale, objectively speaking, is in fact a setting for actions that constitute it as multifarious places by reference to wayful negotiations.

And more than this, for to take that Db as a Db on an Ab way is not merely to have some particular configurational handfulness for that Ab way. It is not merely to have such wayfulness as a contacted appraisal, merely to be moving toward the Db on to an Ab way because of a thumb and turnover move that will follow. The Ab way can be wayfully targeted and wayfully known by a single pointed finger, and with the index digit I can, with eyes closed for example, play an Ab major scale wayfully with competence. I can play a major triad with 'two fingers' arpeggiating it, I can reach with a secure stretch without having the way hoveringly at hand.

My handful knowledge of the terrain is not a knowledge of places that a photograph would depict, and an Ab scale is an Ab *way*, in this terminology, if it is present for 'the hand' for secure targeting: for the 'whole hand,' for 'some of its digits,' for a 'single finger,' and, even more than this, for I can use a pencil to play an Ab scale wayfully. 'Its distances' are known not just to 'fingers,' but to a 'system of spatializations' that may not be reduced to properties of a photographed or filmed characterization (and measurements thereby facilitated). Indeed, the very notion of a way is a *handful* way, not having separable existential properties.*

*This is not to say that 'wayful traverse' may not be studied and that we are reduced to hopelessly mystified conceptions of such bodily phenomena.

I see 'wayful acquisitions' as I watch my beginning piano students first gain facilities at picking out a melody of a song they know. Before having gained skill with playing scales, a was to get to a place where I happened to land, and I got there that way. When doing melodying in the ways I proceeded, merely happening to land on keys was responsible for the extent of my mistakes. To go for that Db definitely would not only be a matter of doing it strongly, with firm pressure, with confidence of aim. It would be to come at it within a course of movements that *finds* the very location of the Db grounded by the locations and configurational requirements of places on the course in which it is wayfully situated-at-hand.

A finely integrated aiming for places, giving

---

hunting and pecking procedure is observed, and the keyboard is a place that has 'its sounds.' Students handfully ask the keyboard for answers to a hopeful intent, rather than display a method with it. They try to find a next note and go too high or low, overcompensate or undercompensate for a next, trying to narrow in on some right tone in between; 'sensing' that a note is much higher they go too much higher, keyboard places having that sort of vagueness which a pitch-dark room has for one trying to find telling places for negotiative passage. The fingers of these beginners display manifold hesitations, holding on to a given note that is now established as in the melody, so as to be able to return to it, finding a place, leaving it, and immediately losing 'its place' when it comes up right away again, and more.

As extensive incorporation of scales occurs, the hand's searching for correct melody tones undergoes progressive wayful elaboration, and the single hunting-pecking finger becomes increasingly part of a 'scale-oriented' appraisal of the terrain. Most melodies are 'constructed' in terms of major scales; wayful acquisition of these scales gradually begins to find the hand arraying itself along 'scale axes'; choices for next notes become progressively integrated with this wayful known-ness of axes of scale territories.

This development can be seen in the developing looks of the searching fingers, as they come to find rather than search; the security of each reach along a way is seen as an emergent acquisition, the reacings proceeding via a way-ed grasp. From the beginning use of a single stabbing-in-the-dark finger—similar to typing with one finger and for the first time in terms of the action's general elegance, but only in that way, for the piano has nothing written on it that tells one about its sounds, with nothing to be relevantly seen—from this stabbing finger, beneath a more-or-less-high-, then more-or-less-low-reaching hand and arm, there emerges a digitally wayful grasp of the soundedness to keys by reference to a course of traversals, would only emerge as a continual possibility in negotiations in the next 'stage' of my jazz studies. And such notions as the definiteness of an aim, the provision of soundedness, the integrated character of a destined course of movements, and the notion of a way essentially at hand await further clarification and exposition as I turn to a new 'element' of my play.

---

contours of the scale. And the competent melody-finder immediately locates that scale within which the melody 'resides.' He is able to 'hear' that scale in knowing the ways so as to find his well-tempered bearing with only a quick first exploration (the well-tempered scaling of modern instruments fashioned by and for bodies with wayful-tempering potentials), and the 'hand' becomes rapidly stanced once that way has been essentially identified.

With further progress, my students' hands show increasingly essentialized wayfulness, where closely hovering appraisals of ways digitally at hand are gradually supplanted. And the hand comes to have melody-finding ways. The process is not unlike the course of essentializings from that point where the beginning typist must hover over the home territory and reach out gingerly for each digit's particular key assignments. He reaches the point where he is doing rapid typings from positions very fluidly sustained in ongoing reconfigurational work well above the keyboard, so that the hands hover over the whole terrain type-ically.

The student concerned with the close investigation of 'wayful acquisitions' as general mobility phenomena of the body may take up, as one example, such a task as picking out a melody. The less experience he has at the keyboard, the more he will find the matter filled with problems. A video taping of several months of such work can be consulted to aid in the 'documentation' and indeed further detailing of such a developmental process, aiding in its further detailing by offering appearances, whose relevance is assessably informed by what the student himself comes to learn at the keyboard. Appearances may be screened for their productional relevance against the background of problematic indications had in the experience, with new potential details made available, through a 'record' so situated, for further interrogation as potential details.

Going for the Jazz

I

More than any single experience, it was listening to Jimmy Rowles play the piano that marked the crucial turning point in my progress toward competent play in the fourth year, and when I reflect upon the most significant changes that began to occur in my ways with the keyboard during this period, this experience epitomizes the nature of the transition.

Jimmy Rowles is something of a musicians' musician, and in the nightclub in Greenwich Village where he worked, jazzmen from all over New York City would gather in their off-hours to hear his marvelous presentations of ballads. He played alone, or with a bass player, and his forte was a most lilting, casual way of playing standard tunes like "Somewhere Over the Rainbow," "Body and Soul," "Tenderly," "The Man I Love." To listen to him was to relish each and every place of a luxuriously lingering song. He was a fine improvisor, but it was the way he played a ballad that commanded so much professional respect.

Jimmy Rowles had a way with the instrument. He sat rather low down and stretched back, almost lazy with the piano like a competent driver is nonchalant behind the wheel on an open road. Still, there was a taking care with the melody, a caressing of it, a giving each place its due. He was never in a hurry; in fact it almost seemed as if he would fall behind the beat, but only seemed that way. It was late-at-night music, and the song would take its time.

I watched him night after night, watched him move from chord to chord with a broadly swaying participation of his shoulders and entire torso, watched him delineate waves of movement, some broadly encircling, others subdividing the broadly undulating strokes with finer rotational movements, so that as his arm reached out to get from one chord to another it was as if some spot on his back, for example, circumscribed a small circle at the same time, as if at the very slow tempos this was a way a steadiness to the beat was sustained.

I would at times watch his chordal hand at work, coming in gently for a landing, and even while staying depressed it seemed to take the chord in passing, never appearing to come to a final rest, as the elbow and arm displayed a course of elliptical rotation around the engaged keyboard hand. As his foot tapped up and down, his head went through a similar rotational course, and the strict up-and-down tapping of the foot was incorporated within a cyclical manner of accenting his bodily movements. In an anchored heel, you could see only the up-and-down movements of the foot, but in the accompanying head rotation and shoulder swaying, you could see a circularly undulating flow of motion, a pushing and releasing, a thrust and relaxation.

At live performances I had watched the very rapid improvisational players whose records had served as my models, but their body idioms in no way seemed connected in detail to the nature of their melodies, and my occasional attempts to emulate the former had no appreciable bearing on my success with the latter. This one, for example, had a little shoulder tic, but mimicking that (which I found myself doing after a night of watching him) did not make his sorts of melodies happen. Another sat tightly hunched over the piano, playing furiously fast, but assuming that posture seemed to have no intrinsic relationship to getting my jazz to happen as his did.

But I found over the course of several months of listening to and watching Jimmy Rowles, and starting to play slow ballads myself (which I had previously done chiefly when first learning chord structures at the very beginning), that in order to get the sound of a song to happen like his, his observable bodily idiom, his style of articulating a beat, served as a guide. In the very act of swaying gently and with elongated movements through the course of playing a song, the lilting, stretching, almost oozing quality of his interpretations could be evoked. It was not that I could imitate his intonations and phrasing with fine success, capture the full richness of his way of moving and pacing and caretaking. His special sense of time was sufficiently distinctive to make him a difficult player to readily imitate. But I found that I could get much of his breathing quality into a song's presentation by trying to copy his ways.

Listening to him, taking notice for the first time of ways of moving at the keyboard, beginning to play slow music, bringing attention for the first time, peculiar as it was and so much a part of my isolation from the occupation, to a careful regard for the presentation of a song, giving that sort of a care to the beat which his bodily idiom displayed, I began to develop a fundamentally different way of being at the piano.

And while at first it was particularly with respect to the presentation of a song that I found a practical relevance to this new attention, progress slowly came with respect to the fast improvisational playing I continued to work at, and within my practice sessions little spates of that jazz on the records unpredictably showed themselves to me, and then disappeared. No sooner did I try to latch on to a piece of good-sounding jazz that would come out in the midst of my improvisations, than it would be undermined, as when one first gets the knack of a complex skill, like riding a bicycle or skiing, the attempt to sustain an easeful manage-

| ment undercuts it. You struggle to stay balanced, keep falling, and then almost suddenly several revolutions of the pedals are sustained with the bicycle seeming to go off on its own, and you try to keep it up, and it disintegrates. But there is no question that the hang of it has been glimpsed, the bicycle seems to do the riding all by itself, and the essence of the experience is tasted. All prior ways of being seem thoroughly lacking, and the new way is encountered with a 'this is it' feeling, almost as a revelation. It was like that.

And a conversation with myself now began to take a certain form, looking down at these hands of mine, their ways, my ways of employing them, seeking practically useful terms for conceiving 'my relationship to their ways,' reflecting upon how I could employ them, and what it meant, as manageable practices at the keyboard, to 'employ them' for this music to happen - a thoughtful scrutiny over such matters, and over the very consequences of the thoughtfulness itself, became a central part of what practicing the piano now came to involve.

My work at the instrument found it an all-or-nothing affair. I would see a stretch of action (melody) suddenly appear, unlike others I had ever seen, and appearing at first, seeming at least, as though the fingers were, because of something I was doing, going places I could not find myself able to see I had specifically taken them. Certain right notes played in certain right ways appeared, in the beginning, in a little spate of play that would go by before I got a good look at it, to just get done. And while I certainly did these notes in these ways, a practically relevant observation was to be progressively realized, in ways of moving I would come to develop, in that strange sort of initial noticing. Watching from above and seeing a stretch of action in a way that would prompt me to say 'look at that, that jazz just came out,' prophesized a way of doing these right notes in right ways

so that they would appear to just come out. This |
sense of being on to something grew from these
witnessings, and my encounters with the hands
would search for that way of proceeding. Small indications of this sort became targets, first glimpses
of what the way of being would have to somehow
achieve.

It was not that a sort of jazz line would appear, something better than another had been, and
then one a bit better still, with gradations that
would reveal readily detectable shifts in a range of
isolatable components of my ways. The distinction
under fleeting regard was not as between a street-
corner conversation and a passage in Rilke, as between the ordinarily competent jazz pianist's solo
and the elegance of a Herbie Hancock improvisation. It was like the difference between the apha-
sic's or stutterer's or brain-damaged speaker's or
new foreigner's attempts to put together a smooth
sentence, and the competent three-year-old's
flowing utterance: Daddy, come see my new doll.
Former ways had been lacking at the level of difference, between features of action that all the
jazz on the records minimally share and the sorts
of struggling amateur efforts that would never pass
for competent play at all. This level becomes my
descriptive concern as it was my practical one.

What happened, suddenly appearing and then
disappearing in these ways, was quite different
from what former practices on the terrain had
amounted to. For a brief course of time while
playing rapidly along, a line of melody would be
generated, interweavingly flowing over the duration of several chords, fluently winding about in
ways I had never seen my hands wind about before, a line of melody whose melodicality was not,
at least it seemed, being expressly done as in my
reiterative attempts to sustain continuities. An
ordering of notes, stating a succession of chords,
being melodic in being of that jazz language, a
language composed of, better: existing as, the

hands' ways of seeming to just move about properly—this was somehow achieved. It was quite
clear that these ways of interweavingly singing jazz
with my fingers, first so difficult to find myself
doing as continuously sustained sayings, were the
ways of that jazz on the records.

There was no mistaking it, no doubt about the
new accomplishment, and I knew no recording of
my play was necessary to check out the assessment, feeling quite certain without inviting a jazz
musician's verification. And I was right. I could
hear it. I could hear a bit of that language being
well spoken, could recognize myself as having
done a saying in that language, in fact, for the first
time, a saying particularly said and particularly
said in all its details: its pitches, intensities, pacing, durations, accentings—a saying said just so.

The particularly said jazz sayings would be
done, and then I would lapse into usual lunge-ful
and unsingingly path-following ways. The practical
theorizings, searching for instructions that would
work, made up a course of several months of now
almost continuous play, getting close and not
wanting to let the changes recede, trying to nail
matters down firmly so that I could do it again. It
was the sort of affair where at first many days of
regular playing might not produce a single instance, and months went by before I could play an
entire chorus of this jazz of the records. The pro-
tracted struggle was the source of frustration as it
kept alive various problematics of the production,
making possible their examination and description
here, a payoff I came to appreciate only after the
fact.

I always knew when the right appearances
were being displayed, knowing it in the so familiar
sounds of the records, and knowing it also in the
very looks of the hands. For now I saw jazz piano
players' hands a bit at a time and would recall
other piano players' hands. I would see, in mine
now, looks that were closely reminiscent of ways I

had often seen but not studied in others. As my |
hands' looks looked as their's had looked, I recol-
lected the looks of their's with refined detail.
Things passingly seen in the others' hands were
oddly clarified, in hindsight, through looks mine
now passingly began to seemingly reveal to me,
and this remembrance would itself prove to
eventually be most helpful. That puzzling inter-
weavingness of my teacher's hands, whose order,
the order of the music, I could not formerly see,
looking beyond them for rules about their destinations—this, for example, was spotted in mine.

Though it at first appeared to be a slight shift,
appearing this way because it would either happen
right or not, with very little in between, the real
jazz presenting itself so dramatically special and
with nothing that I could precisely nail down as
things to do, I could not practically reduce the accomplishment to ways that would make it just
happen by trying out this or that slight shift. That
was like trying out a shoulder tic I had witnessed in
some other's play. Instructions that would work
had to break down the seemingly uncontrollable
accomplishment into some particular practices,
and my playing sessions searched the appearances—these sounds and hands' looks—for guides
to formulate principles. A practical analysis of
what was happening was needed to yield this and
that in particular I could tell myself to do to get
that jazz to just happen.

Playing the piano now, playing for some
friends or in a nightclub, it occurs after no more
than several instants at the keyboard that I find
myself singing. I sing with my fingers. One may
sing along with the fingers, one may use the fingers
to blurt out a thought, and one may sing with the
fingers. There are specific differences in ways of
being singingly present with the fingers and the terrain to be identified here.

When I found, in my new play, a long line of
interweaving melody just coming out over the dur-

ation of several chords, I found myself doing a saying in that language, a saying particularly said in all its details. And I was doing singing, often aloud while playing, and now found, on such rather fleeting first occasions, that a new way of being singingly present had emerged. I gradually found instructions that could helpfully be brought to operational use with respect to this presence, as I came to understand the keyboard ways it entailed. And, in turn, I found I understood such ways in finding an instruction that helped, any understanding having that test for me at the piano. Instructions that helped about singing with the fingers began to figure into a generalized mode of guided presence at the terrain, well integrating with other helpful practices I could begin to locate, other features of my play I could understand and instruct the hands about.

Consider using the fingers to blurt out a thought, prominent in my earlier repetitional lungings. When typing very rapidly at the typewriter, I sometimes engage in an investigation, finding problems of 'improvisational writing' informing and informed by problems of improvisational piano playing, involving, among other practices, this:

I proceed very rapidly, without the use of a text, striving to make real sayings, sensible ones, expressing 'ideas' we say, seeking to sustain a pace to the proceedings that approximates that of rather slow but not terribly uncommon conversational speaking. Doing such typing and trying to continue to proceed without any undue amount of pausing, exploring problems of improvisational negotiations through this terrain, it often happens that I come to a place where I cannot reach further. My movements are not broadly aimed up ahead, lack ways that reach forward in certain malleable, improvisationally flexible, accentually targeted thrusts, and at such times it also happens that I find myself sensing that I cannot find what to be saying next.

And I aim to keep typing nonetheless, as though having to continuously produce 'sayables' for an audience, sayables that come and then disappear, like the sayings of talk come and go, imposing that constraint by using video tapings that focus closely on the typewriter carriage.

In such finger talking I find myself coming upon a loss for words as my hands begin to halter and lack surety in their forward sweep, and sensing such difficulty just up ahead, I frequently say a group of words, trying to get myself out of trouble, trying to do this while typing fast nonetheless. I often prefigure a little stretch of places to aim for, going fast this way and feeling an impasse coming up, taking an inner course of action to help the outer one out, it may be metaphorically said, and in such searchings a course of words may be sometimes done in a flash. I may image several words, say them at a flash to myself, doing one or the other or both with that sort of rapidity that thinking to oneself can have, and find, doing so while typing along, attempting such prefiguring without pausing as other sayables are being fingered, that I may lunge for the group of words all at once.

Lunging for a group of words all at once, possible for thinking, would be communicatively usable in a world where talking occurred with the sorts of actions the postal clerk employs when stamping AIR MAIL SPECIAL DELIVERY on your letter with one blow. But in presently organized affairs, sequential articulations of the body make up such matters as talking and writing and melodying, and to lunge for a group of words all at once, with fingers at the typewriter or the articulatory apparatus of the mouth (the word 'apparatus' not without some troublesome connotations), is to produce garbled-looking sayables or garbled-sounding sayings. The production must be linearized. I may think in words given all at once, doing what has been called a 'monothetic thought' (not that it is without a duration and hence sequential in that way), but when I move my fingers over the typewriter, doing finger talking, or move my mouth, I must say each next 'letter' or each next 'sound' in serial order.

Finding myself in a jam, trying to do a thoughtful saying, finding trouble flowing backwardly through the forwardly ill-aimed reach of the hands, lunging for a group of words produces a garbled-looking sayable, one that often contains within it bits and pieces of the thought words that were lunged for, as the fingers reach as though stamping out the thought, and many errors are generated.

And in that form of being singingly present when I tried to use the fingers to blurt out an elaborate note passage, as in my earlier reiterative attempts to do melodying by duplicating a prior figure, the consequences of the lunge produced, for the music, an order of disarray, speaking from the fingers' standpoint, 'equivalent' to the disarrayed sights I get in such lunged finger talking here.

Then there is that form of typing where one may sustain an ongoing course of thought as the typing, not doing any inner sayings or imaginings with words apart from the fingers' movements, where a strict synchrony is sustained between any sayings you may be saying to yourself and the movements of the fingers. Doing that sort of typing can occur with few pauses on occasion, and quite fluently, and one is then singing with the fingers.

The things I formerly had to say were not the sorts of sayings to say, for lunging would not work, or, to put it better, the jazz on the records I aimed for is not filled with lunges of the sort I had made, with many notes merely landed upon. It is constituted of sayings that are particularly accomplishable, each and every next sounding place expressly aimed for and arrived at, while mine had been composed of 'sounds,' looking at the music from without, that were the consequences of a very unevenly sustained singingness. I would be in and out of gear with these hands and the soundable terrain, almost trying to stamp out a prior figure in a new context.

A specific instruction was: take directions from the positional locale and readiness of the hands in choosing notes to soundfully say. With my hand in this position

I have here, just at hand, a host of soundful places to take the fingers for all the chords of a song. An entire solo can be well performed without extensive venturing, and I can play notes that accord well, so to speak, with the song's ongoing harmonic progression, from such a territory of tones in the immediate handful neighborhood of such a scope.

To instruct myself: take singing directions from the positional locale and readiness of the hands, both took cognizance as it helped make workable the realization of such a possibility, understandings and practices coupled as they were in this fashion.

Before I had proceeded in little chord-by-chord stretches of action, and while I had worked out some few routes that accorded well, theoretically speaking, with a progression of chords, there were few of these at hand, few worked-out solutions for continuously traveling from one smoothly available and characteristic jazz-sounding path, like a diminished scale, onto another rapidly traversable and chord-specific path, without interruption.

Playing along fast on one route and finding the next chord coming up, I found the need to switch routes, and while I could by this point employ some of the paths from various starting points—from top to bottom, coming in at the middle, playing portions of a route like every other note, from the top, bottom, or middle—going fast in the ways I went fast, it always felt required to prefigure the route onto which I would switch when the next chord's arrival was imminent.

It was some time since it had been as frantic a searching up ahead as in my first year of play, since a conceptual procedure of chord-route matchings was explicitly experienced as a naming process in my thinking, as at first. But accompanying my play was considerable imaging of routes and their layouts, and where I was in the terrain, and this imaging was on occasion ahead of where my fingers were, to aid in a transition when moving along rapidly and feeling the encroaching arrival of a next chord in the song.*

*The beginning typist may find himself spelling every word as he types, thinking the spelling of the words as a step-by-step search of the looking fingers for correct places. The advanced typist may make it through an unaccustomed passage by conceiving the fingers doing the spelling, not so as to 'remember' where the proper characters lie through an image of the terrain, but so as to make it through an unfamiliar sight in the text being copied. The wheres of the fingers and the terrain here assume a renewed significance for a moment. Specific finger-character responsibilities are not imaged, they having long since been forgotten (and indeed many typists must go through a mimicked fingering of words on an imagined terrain in order to fill out a diagram of the typewriter's named places). But that the terrain is a 'place for spelling' now becomes, in such unaccustomed passages, a part of the typist's entire way of approaching the keyboard. The hands behave spellingly, gearing up with a precision of stance that is more characteristic of the beginner's way of staying in close hovering proximity to the home territory, to help move assuredly through the definitive transportation of a troublesome sight.

Now I may play rapidly along, singing the jazz with my fingers, fully involved in a singing being particularly said, caught up in the music. At the same time, indeed in precise synchrony, I may without looking at the keyboard visualize the notes being played, the names of the notes, seeing the spellings of the melodies. The same sort of synchrony, it could be suggested, between my 'visualizations' and my 'singings,' occurs here, at the typewriter, in relations obtaining between the sayings I may say to myself as I type and the movements of my fingers. If I say something ahead of where the fingers are, I will make an error. And if I speak aloud while typing along with my sayings, as the articulations occur we may hear-see that the fingers are proceeding through just those places on this terrain that correlate, in this integrated bodily reaching system, to the places my mouth parts traverse in doing the sayings being typed.

It can be suggested that the sights of a text-being-copied may not deserve the designation 'sayables.' From the typist's standpoint a text's sights are rather differently constituted than from a reader's. I have found that in fairly short order I can type from a foreign-language text whose sights I cannot say at all, though a productive research question can be posed: how does the 'sayability' of a sight figure into typed reproduction nonetheless? After practice at typing Czech for some while, gaining an increasingly finer mobile grasp of some of its characteristic looks as spelled affairs, and moves, as typewriter courses, I am still far from my usual speed in reproducing English sights. Would much more practice decrease or eliminate such a discrepancy? Word-sights-seen-to-be-typed are seen with looking reaches that may not require a grasp that appreciates an unfolding sensibility, and the looking that reproducing a text requires may not be at all suited to such appreciations. Its pacing structure, for one thing, is not that which makes up part of the work of normal reading, not because it is slower, but because it has a different organization of forward thrusting to integrate well with the task at hand. Yet the recognizability of the sights-seen-to-be-typed may involve something more than a reach over a surveyable landscape for the competent native typist. The sayability of the sights, and perhaps their sense (in the ways a sense might be gesturally had in typing-looking), enters into the accomplishment in ways whose study could lead us to learn more about 'reading,' 'looking,' and 'understanding.'

As I type a lengthy word, having to speak at
that peculiarly elongated pace that speaking as I
type (or write longhand) involves, I enunciate the
various syllables, stretching the course of mouth
movements, in slow motion right along with the
syllables being done with the fingers, in strict synchrony. The two go together as two hands proceed
together to reach for a package, each getting to its
side of the parcel, however differently distanced
the sides are from the hands' locations when the
move begins, going together toward their destinations and arriving on time together.

Looking down at the hands and finding a spate
of that jazz coming out, I would find that I was
looking to the hands and now seeing ways of traverse apart from the notes being chosen. Where
before I had looked past the hands' ways to their
destinations, when a spate of that jazz was spotted
my look now at times shifted back, the focal plane
seemingly coming closer, and I would see a configurating hand, in a certain arrangement with respect
to the keys, whose shaping was now being
watched, whose shaping and movings became
gradually instructable, as what was seen here
became grasped with further clarity, and vice-
versa.

I began to see and then find use for further
work in the observation that note choices could be
made anywhere, that there was no need to lunge,
that usable notes for any chord lay just at hand,
that there was no need to find a path, image one
up ahead to get ready in advance for a blurting out.
Indeed, to conceive particular terrain places up
ahead seriously undermined the singing that I
sought to sustain. Good notes were everywhere at
hand, right beneath the fingers. I found, for example, that where it before seemed required to reach
for a big path for a chord, foreseeing its locale and
organizational requirements with a 'monothetic
hand,' a single note would do to make melody over
the course of several chords' durations. I could

take my time in going for a long run, could linger, |
finding right beneath a nonventuring hand all sorts
of melodying possibilities, if I lingered there in the
right ways. And when doing venturing in the right
ways I could move fast and take my time both together, not contradictory possibilities, as descriptions to follow indicate.

One note could be played during one chord's
duration and another note, 'right next to it,' played
for another's, and a melody could be done as such
doings. Of course I knew that as a child playing
"Jingle Bells," but the jazz had more than anything
else appeared as this fast-flowing rapidity, this
seemed its essence; to do that was for me to have
become a jazz musician, and in the solos I listened
to it was always the 'hardest' passages that were my
goals. I had not problematically heard those plen-
tiful examples on the records of sparsely textured
and nonventuring melodies, always attending
doings going on all over the keyboard.

I began to employ the melodic hand in ways
to let it then speak to me about the sort of shaping
it was in, the sort of stance over the sector being
adopted. I could take directions from the fingers
about ways of moving and where to move, avoiding lunging's troubles, and at the same time, because of this caretaking and my characteristic
sounding routes, jazz melodies began to be seen
and heard. I could venture when ready to do so,
and not, if I so wished, making jazz melodies both
ways, such a variability to my play being part of
what using the hands requires and achieves in the
sounds of this music.

A new sort of hookup between the singing me
and these hands was developing, a new way of
being singing with the fingers emerging, as next
sounds I would project began to come under the
mutual jurisdiction of the positional array of the
hands. I began to join up in a new partnership with
the hands and the sounding terrain, as where we
were going together began to slowly integrate into

an altogether new way of doing singing at the piano: a new way for intentions to be formed, a new sort of synchrony and directionality of linkage between my head's aimings for sung sounds and my fingers' aiming for singable sounds, becoming progressively shaped and refined.

II

Recall my earlier lungings, getting part of my saying definitely said and then merely happening to land upon 'any notes thereabout.' In an important sense everything had been amiss. I would play a figure and reach for a reiteration, move for a restatement in another setting, one appropriately located, I then felt, for this figure's statement con-chordant with the harmonic progression.

What it had been was a course of movements, accomplished in the chord-alloted time, and a next chord was coming up that would have its durational tenure, and the pitching shape of the course was reached for in the next sector, to be accomplished during the next chord's durational stay. The chords go by: 1, 2, (change), 3, 4, (change), 1, 2 . . . .

And the course of movements with its pitched shape was composed of thus and so many notes. I tried to transport it in its entirety to the new place, and would set out into the reiteration with so many notes to get done there, would often get the beginning well placed, and feel obliged, transporting it in its entirety, to say as many more notes as were required. It had so much to it, to be done again.

A pace had been given to the original statement, a pace that, when adhered to over the alloted time, would bring it through a particular number of notes, and this particular number of notes had to be done again for it to be repeated. To do melodying with the whole of it, making the whole of it relate to something then done, and

something then done relate backwardly to it, I |
entered into the new sector at an initial pace and
way of pacing that committed me to carry out a
line of action of just that many notes to do the
whole of it.

But, you will recall, I was often in shape to get
the beginning part of it successfully reiterated, but
not able to singingly aim for the rest of it. I lost
grasp of its shaping because of configurational
changes required to do it equivalently in the territory. I lost my grasp because of different shapings
required of the hand, new fingerings that I could
not accommodate to in rapid course, turn-under
arrangements posed by the new place that, with a
moment's reshifting, I (my hand) might have been
able to take account of, had I given myself a moment.

But I did not. I went into the repeating attempt with a paced course of note passage initially
established with the pace of the opening two finger
moves that committed me to do the whole of it,
with just so many notes, in the alloted chordal
time. And losing handful grasp over its restatement, having set up that sort of pace that committed me to the whole number of notes of it before
the new chord's durational tenure would expire, I
would often play these any notes thereabout, and
finish up the whole of it with just so many of them.
Having set out in paced ways that would have
made stopping short of just so many of them often
likely to have made me trip, the hand literally
going faster than it could keep its balance in the
new sector to get those pitches done; setting out in
paced ways that would have compounded the experienced loss of grasp over the attempted saying
with a stopping-short trip; I would instead often
produce a just-so-many course of unsung non-
sense notes. I would get the fingers down somewhere to preserve at least the whole amount of it
without tripping on top of everything else. Often it
would work like this:

I would get started into the reiteration a bit late, because perhaps the lunge was a big one, or involved a slight preparatory reconfiguration to get to the new locale in a possibly workable shape for the accomplishment to happen there. Or the prior figure itself, it too being pacedly aimed from the beginning in such a way as to imply a certain number of notes be played in the reaching being made, might go a trifle longer than its chord duration. This would delay the transition, or require a shifting movement to the new place even faster. I would often start a touch late into the new sector to do a melody, would sometimes speed up the pace to get the whole of it down before the new chord came or, in starting out late, would run a trifle over into the next chord's temporal reign.

At times a grab for this next chord would be held up ever so slightly, the left hand's reach trying to accommodate the rating of the right's articulations, so that the two might participate in stating some beat together, keeping the song tempoed. Such an accommodation did not often lend the impression of a beat missed altogether, was not so pronounced as to sound as though I could not keep time, but enough so that the flow of the proceedings was out of kilter ever so slightly. And when a flow of articulatory proceedings is pacingly out of kilter ever so slightly, what is said can be thrown into the most massively disorganized appearance. An ever so slightly ill-paced reach may not be at all recognizable as that melody; and articulational reachings improperly targeted ahead may not only make what is being said obscure, but may produce a course so disorganized as to make it unclear that it is of some particular language at all, even that it is of a language as we know them.

The joint reachings of my left and right hands were out of kilter, usually because of the pacing character of the right's articulating moves (for I seldom did much left-hand obliging, feeling the song's harmonic intactness to be beat-fully retained at all costs as a most prominent requirement

for adherence to the format). The chord would be |
reached for with the left hand, and the right hand's
melodying reaches would start out and end as best
they could during the necessary interims. Not
doing much left-hand-pace obliging, it was nonetheless the case that left-hand reachings were often
less than solid in their accentually aimed grabs,
movings going on with the right having their way,
in and through the body, of upsetting the pace of
mobilities on the left side (and of course vice-
versa).

The out-of-kilter relationship between the two
hands was at times as in the ill-jointedness of two
workers' moves in lifting a heavy package, where,
because of a slight difference in the acceleration-
al-decelerational shape of each's respective uplift-
ing thrusts, the object comes off the ground tilted
down at the heavy end, for example. The worker at
that end, having to heave with more accentual
force than the other, perhaps not having assessed
the parcel's weight or the distance to be traversed
(or the other having perhaps failed with respect to
his transporting requirements) is usually the one
who shouts: "Hold it a minute. Now, again: ready,
set, go."

Often the trouble happens in the first instance
because their 'ready, set, go' lacks that sort of
pacing shape, as a course of moves itself, which is
coordinationally suited for the task at respective
hands; or because while it has a workable thrusting
form for one's task it does not for the other's; or a
'ready, set, go' suited to both is done a bit privately
by each and not with adequate concertedness.

The ready of my reachings was not the right
kind of a ready, and the instruction to choose
places to go by looking to the positional readiness
of the hands, part of this singing with the fingers,
was helpful in being appreciative of and useful in
instituting the ways of aiming that were required:
paced aims that would lend to the place achieving
moves that sort of fine internal temporal layout
that makes such courses jazz melody courses.

I would reach for a course of places for each chord at a time, the forward extent of my reach abbreviated as a course of articulations that would come to an end, somehow, somewhere, for each chord. The reaching was toward an 'ahead' posted before or upon the next chord's arrival time, to enable a switch. It was not a reach toward an ahead that would take a course of moves up to and through the next chord's durational tenure, or still further ahead, several chord grabs 'up the way.'

I reached for interim arrival times and ill-defined arrival times at that, rather than for long interchordal stretches of melodying that would have a jazz ordering in winding about through the statement of a sequence of chords. I reached for melodies as the new walker gets across the room by lunging first for the leg of the coffee table, then his mother's, then to the bottle at the end of the couch.

The chord-grabbing reaches, done with that sort of 'singingness' you give to the sounds of your feet when you walk while conversing with another, hardly any singing at all, were securely targeted moves. But there was not a doing something with something already done, as when you walk to expressly make a march happen in the taps of your steps. The chordal reaches were not bringing forward something done into something next done as a singing affair. They were securely targeted reaches but not soundful, in not being of an unfolding melodicality, and for the chords to become part of a melody in their own right, courses of interchordal melodying would be required for them to receive soundful status.

And along with such chordal walking reaches rather than marchingly sung steps, themselves sometimes slightly ragged, I reached with the right hand for courses of articulation step by step—from coffee table to mother's leg, from this intersection just to that one, from this phrase   to this one
        and then to this (but not in ways that would

produce such normal-looking sayables in 'live' fin- |
ger talking). I reached step by step rather than as
through the apartment looking for a toy, as quickly
across town to pick up a package, as right through
the production of a sentence as the one I am now
typing, were you able to see it, very quickly,
moving straight ahead as I proceed, finding myself
in difficulties but knowing at the pace I am now
moving at, however little is being said well, however rambling things are going . . . (I lost it.)

You can lose the thought—and I did not mean
to say *pace* but *pacing way*—in very rapid typing,
in very rapid talking (and in slow typing and talk as
well, of course), depending upon the sorts of
interwoven courses you seek to generate, and may
have to take stock. But with the format of a fixed
set of chords always coming up, you do not lose
your way in the same ways. There is always an orderly course to unite the proceeding, a format to
give you places toward and through which to
reach, these chordal landmarking targets.

Having a chord progression is like having the
speaking task of giving a stranger instructions on
how to get from here to there, in the hometown
you know so well: through the course of the instructions there are places you must sayingly lead
the other through to get to the end; there is the
destination at the end that the instructions must
come to, with benchmarks along the way, say in
the intersectional course you must outline in sequence to get from here to there. And in such sayings you find the particular ways to tell him about
the best way from this standardly employed intersection to that standardly employed intersection,
finding the particular courses of movements to
sayingly lead him across town in the usual ways
one gets from here to there, in the course of the directions.

But my reaches—aphasically targeted step by
step and not broadly aimed ahead through several
then sung chordal landmarks, to bring off a course

of jazz-ordered, sentential interweavings—were in their own ways spastic. And articulationally spastic reaches produce, for a reach of even quite short duration, a coordinational trouble in making the next step happen well. They produce a course of movements with temporal disarray throughout, a course without that pacing ordering that makes the articulated place achievements a saying of that language.

An articulationally spastic reach produces, for the smooth and joint recognizability of the course, a trouble akin to the workers' coordinational difficulties, and may well arise as it did in my piano playing out of an ill-formed shaping of a ready-set-go, of continually formed ready-set-goes.

I would in my repeating attempts go for a bunch of notes, to get them down before or at the time of the next chord's statement, before or along with the landing of the left hand at its next temporarily achieved place of vaguely sounding repose. I would go for a bunch of notes, reaching for a completion by then, but the first production and the attempted reproduction were both lacking in the ways they were prospectively oriented to a time of arrival by then.

So many notes had to be played, and these so many notes lay in a terrain of places whose shaping and dimensions were known, by reference to the hand's territorial and distancing commands, as a setting of places-at-hand. So many places-at-hand had to be played with a pacing course whose rating was established at the outset to try to get the whole of the preceding melody out by then. And the places were not at hand, in the ways they needed to be available, to get so many of them to happen by then. They were not singingly at hand in ways they needed to be, not chosen in the first instance through an organization of moving that would enable reaching so many places singingly selected in course by then. The places were prechosen without respect for the singable-at-handness-of-so-many-by-then.

And the most significant problem was that in- |
stead of lunging for so many prechosen, variously
located, unsingable, ill-at-hand places by then,
trying to stamp out bunches of melody, what I
should have been doing was getting the then-ness
of my reaching aims together, choosing paces for
travel to get thus and so many singable notes found
in course. I should have been moving with an articulational aim toward a together-then-ness. The
most relevant instruction generated out of such
witnessings, and aiding in bringing such matters
under handful employment, was: get the beat into
the fingers and do not let it merely be the foot and
left hand's work. And more broadly: establish a
firmly recurrent accentual beating 'everywhere,'
and not just a somewhat straggling though time-
keeping tap of the foot, with a more or less coordi-
nated course of grabbing reaches with the left hand
as the right went fast and jazzily.

I needed firm prospectivities for arrival as the
workers need a firm pulse that tells them when 'go'
is to be done, and tells them when the next node of
the pulse (unstated but bodily implied by the shaping of the preceding 'ready, set') is to be done, so
that they know not only where they are going but
when they must get there. Knowing when they
must get there enables them to pace the course of
the differently distanced movements toward there
smoothly, 'smoothness' defined in terms of the requirements posed by the tasks at hands. In jazz
and language sayings, smoothness must be formulated in terms of that fine internal pacing structure
of the articulations that furnishes their recognizable cogency.

To get the time into the fingers, hands, shoulders, everywhere, was to develop mobile ways with
the terrain such that commitments to arrival times
could be continuously altered and shifted about in
the course of the negotiations, a steady beat to the
song as a whole sustained all the while. It was to
aid in having sayings always at hand for any pacings, always known to be singingly up ahead in any

venturings, without having to know the particular wheres up ahead through any prefiguring. It was to permit nonstuttering and nontripping disengagements from the terrain when a saying was not at hand, disengagements that would not make the music stop but would be silences of the music.

Watching Jimmy Rowles, I had come home and begun moving by setting a tempo in new ways. Before, when in group play or alone, I had counted a 1, 2, 3, 4 more suited for counting a series of numerals from 1 to 20 than for making music, and now I began to do a 1 and 2 and 1 2 3 4, setting a tempo with a rotating cyclical movement with strong forward thrusts. Now instead of keeping a beat as one may tap with rigid up-and-down finger-confined moves on the table, I began to count off the time with finger-snapping, head-bobbing, arm-and-shoulder rotating courses having little elliptical shapings: push and push and push and push. And more than that, I began to state a beat, as the forward thrusts of my body and especially the right hand and fingers, with a 1 2 3 4 1 2 3 4 1 2 3 4 1 2 3 4, an accenting and not just a pulse. I began to do at the piano, and with my 'right side' particularly, the sort of accentual moves many listeners do, the sort of accentual thrusting I had always done in listening to music, whether that music be jazz with its class of accentual ways, or Beethoven with its, or the Beatles with 'their's': whether it be a strong thrust or gentle sway, a syncopated or jointly aimed move, an abrupt thumping or gliding flow of ups and downs, the thrusts of marchings' aims or minuets', the reaches for a long course of sayings up to an accentual thrust just *now*, or for 'daddy, come here'—with firm prospectivities.

And for improvisational negotiations it was not enough that the beat be my foot's work. It had to come into the hand. I would see it come into the hand when I came home from an evening watching him, got lazy and low down with the piano, and

found the entire right hand beginning to do accentually thrusted courses of movement. During
pauses I sometimes watched the tempo being
tapped out with little forward thrusts on the front
of tiny circles at the fingertips, above or even ever
so slightly on the keys, never sounding one eventually, unless I sang it, with thus and such an accented and paced move into the terrain, sprung off
those tiny circles at the fingertips; unless I sang it
just so just now and just then.

It would be found coming into the arms and
shoulders as well, the shoulders, for example, in
light of the relationships between the two hands.
The chord-grabbing reach must do its stretching
with correspondingly firm accentual thrusts, as the
fingers skip an accent, which they would come to
do, heading instead for a longer succession of
notes. And the hand now found, without looking
ahead, that it was in shape to take a longer reach,
for just so many yet largely unknown places singingly up until some further ahead accentual node.
Pacing an articulational stretch toward an inter-
chordally ahead accentual node, with an expan-
sion of the temporal prospectivity through a deemphasis in one accent, elongating the move toward
an accent up ahead: $\underline{1}$ 2 3 4 $\underline{1}$ 2 3 4 $\underline{1}$ 2 3 4 $\underline{1}$ 2 3 4 —
skipping an accent in a reach for a longer stretch,
the chord grabbing and now soundful reach would
breathe for the right. And now the solidly rocking
back and shoulders helped tell it, as the two hands
'lifted this package' together, when and how to
take a breath, and where a breath could be taken
quickly without upsetting the right hand's accentually targeted and elongated place achievements.
The beat would come into, gain accentual constitution by, this participation of the shoulders and
back, in a joint enterprise of soundful sayings, and
this participation would come to be achieved in
time without any detectable movements doing this
pulse solidly in the back and shoulders, everywhere. So would the beat come into my ways.

Watching Jimmy Rowles doing things like that, pieces of that jazz would appear in my emulations. Before characterizing what this new mobile hand would do and become as an improvisatory organ under my instructions; how this strongly established, prospective accentual node would figure into soundful place finding in course; would figure into doing long reaches toward further ahead accents; would enable systematic ways of skipping and shifting accents about that were firmly there; would figure centrally into reachings for long interchordal passages singingly; would involve doing reiterations and repetitions and other melodying practices in altogether new fashions now—before doing some further keyboard detailing, I should like to give a brief sketch of some general observations made about 'pulsing' and 'accenting.'

Trying to take a close look at what a pulsing is, I encountered considerable difficulties arising out of 'problems' of seeing, measuring, and defining body time keeping. But despite these 'problems of data reduction' most especially, deriving from such facts as that a pulsing may be nowhere clearly in sight so as to study its organization as a seen phenomenon, a few primitive observations were made. Call them: topics for further research. There were 'troubles' in seeing a body pulsing. When, for example, drawing a spiral in the way once required of grade-schoolers when good script was important (before IBM and the telephone), where a recurring thrust is made on the downstroke side—with a rhythm not unlike that of various styles of improvised jazz:

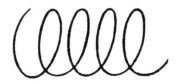

a strong push may not 'show up' at all clearly as varying intensities in the resultant path. The arm and shoulder, for example, may rotate more markedly during the thrusting stages (without this being readily seen), taking pressure off the pencil, so that one may be doing an accented course and get a spiral that appears to have been produced with an even pacing and pressure throughout.

Despite these 'troubles,' whether in spirals being accentually drawn or in moves of the body itself being watched, some topics for further research, which will have to 'cope' with such 'troubles,' were noticed in some amateur experiments I did. I sketch them quickly, to then turn to the hands' new ways, noticing such findings because I have found that my efforts to further detail jazz-productive, instructable practices at the keyboard are provisionally enriched by observations made using the resources of primitive clock measurements.

I draw two dots: •   • and set myself the task of connecting them with a line, while at the same time tapping with a finger on the table. I constrain myself so that I will arrive at the second dot as the tapping finger reaches the table. I set out in one of two ways to achieve this coordination. I either begin the movement of the line as the finger rises off the table from a prior beating:

or I begin the line when the finger is at the top of an upstroke, starting on the way down:

If I start out the line drawing when the finger is already on its way up, or when somewhere in the midst of the downstroke:

I cannot smoothly bring the line to the next dot in conjunction with the finger's achievement of the table. I do not know how fast to move, and I must hold up one or another of the movements and bring the two into alignment. I employ a common pulsing to unite the two differentially distanced moves (the reader may easily verify this observation).

The smoothest accomplishment of the pencil's reach in concordance with the finger's tapping occurs when I start both gestures out together. The finger begins the tapping move, now rises after a tap is made, oriented toward an upswing, turn-around, and descent that will bring it back to the table for the next tap. A pulsing has been established and a next tap is approached.

As the tapping finger rises, prospectively so oriented, adjusting its rate of movement by reference to the distance to be traversed before the next tap's time of arrival, the line drawing sets out. It is now prospectively oriented with the tapping finger

toward a time of arrival in common, at each's destination. In slow-motion filming, one can find a
definition of smoothness in this coordination, furnished by the resultant acceleration-deceleration
patterns.* The line drawing proceeds, when coordinating to an even pulsing, and when constrained
as on the edge of a ruler to involve a straight path,
by first accelerating, as is required from a standstill
position, then reaching a constant speed, and then
decelerating on the approach to the second dot,
lest it be overshot. When a pulsing is evenly maintained and with no accentual one-sidedness (see
below), in terms of body evenness, which shows,
when compared to the clock, some rather stable
regularities—which can be taken to signify that the
clock was well designed in terms of the body and
its mathematics—the straight line shares, with the
finger-tapping course, a turnaround from acceleration to deceleration that both gestures have in
common. The line starts out quickly; halfway
through the duration of the interval it has reached
a constant speed, and then begins a deceleration.
The finger tapping reaches a turnaround from the
upbeat to the downbeat halfway through its course
as well.

Each gesture has a distance to traverse, a
speed to attain, and a rate of acceleration to attain
that speed, and the speeds and rates of acceleration vary from one gesture to the other. But they
have in common a turnaround, maximum phase,
halfway through.

When I draw two straight lines between dots
like this:

(•   •) (•   •)

using one hand for each reach, and do an even and
relatively unaccented pulsing with my foot, must

---

*I filmed line drawings and finger tappings with a high-
speed camera. These were projected on a blackboard with an
analyst projector, frame by frame, distances from each 1/100
of a second 'interval' to the next marked on the board, such
distances then measured.

reach each destination together and as the foot reaches the floor, the first line connects closely spaced dots, travels more slowly; the second moves quickly. Both gain maximum speed and retain a constant speed midway through:

(Each slash represents 'one unit of time' in these schematizations.)

The interbody work of pulsing has already been suggested in the 'worker' example. Each adjusts the thrust of his movements by aiming toward the upcoming time of arrival, established by the preceding count, appraising the speed required to manage the weight and distance traverse, adjusting the force and extent of the move accordingly, holding these 'variables' in a delicate bodily balance. And their joint pulsing joins their respective moves, in accordance with essentially the same phasing structure that unites the drawing of two lines of different lengths (although particular patterns of acceleration and deceleration are variable with respect to the nature of the task).

When you reach for a doorknob, it is there before you, so far away, a far-away judged by the body's spatialities, and you set out for a rate of movement. You must begin with an extent of push, accelerating, faster than you will sustain, unless you want to swiftly grab or hit the knob. The rate of travel, its accelerations, decelerations, and attained speed are variable with respect to the nature of the activity. You may start out with a quick thrust and then markedly slow down right away. But doing so for many reaches (with a stable target, for if one moves closer as the other reaches to caress, it becomes a punch, with apologies due

and often difficult to allocate) defines one version
of a spastic course of movements, is disruptive to
balance and accomplishment of a reaching task,
and in many circumstances downright dangerous.
One may spastically make one's way around with
mistimed reaches for varieties of actions, but such
a manner of proceeding will be seen, the consequences directly appreciated, and when it comes
to generating a course of articulations, as in music
or talking for others, the pacing of these articulations must be held together so as to flow properly,
so as to produce a course of linguistically proper
movements. It is here that a prospective time of
arrival serves a central organizational role in the
body's movements.

Consider the following situation. I am to play
some notes starting as my foot comes off the floor
and moving until it reaches the floor again, with a
pulsing rate established by a prior tap, so that the
time of arrival of the projected tap is prospectively
given. Instead of drawing a line, I enter the keyboard or tap on a table, and the last tap of the sequence, let us say, must occur coincident with the
next beating. A distanced reach is present here,
with a course of articulations 'situated within' it.

Consider the last note of the sequence. A
reach will have to be made, traversing a distance,
that simultaneously achieves this last note as the
foot returns to the floor. The same basic organization found in the line-drawing suggestion is present
here. I cannot begin the last reach except by integrating its organization with the flow of the beating. If I begin the reach for the last note as the foot
has already begun its final thrust, somewhere in
the midst of this course, I cannot achieve simul-
taneity of arrival.

If I sustain an evenly accented pulsing, which
does not stress the downbeat more than the upbeat, I take a course of movement that may be
schematically indicated as follows:

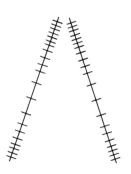

Counting with this beating, I would not give stress to the 'one' count alone, but would count *1 & 2 & 3 & 4 &*, giving equal stress to each swing, and my tapping here assumes the cyclicality of a pendulum:

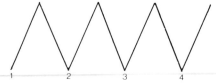

We have here not a 'rhythmic structure,' with recurrent forms of distributive accents, but merely a 'pulsing.' And accenting is, from the standpoint of bodily movements, a move that proceeds with some thrust; when I reach for a note I strive toward a desired intensity of sound, coming in with a strong stroke or with a let-up that will subdue the intensity. Here is a schematized portrayal of an accenting given on the downbeating, and one with upbeating organization:

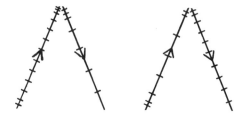

In coordinating a number of articulations to end on a tap, a turnaround phase in the beat-

ing—that 'area' when the deceleration of the up- |
beating phase ceases and a steady speed is
sustained (or the phase comes to a virtual standstill)—need not occur at the 'top' of the foot's
movement. We can have a trajectory that looks
like this:

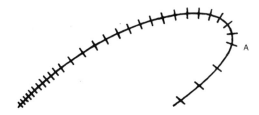

where a course takes an apparently uniform turnaround (in cases when a change of direction is
involved), and the accelerational thrust occurs just
before the contact occurs. There is a long even
stretch with a hurry-up at the end.

To say that I must begin the reach for the last
note of a sequence, articulated between two beat-
ings when the downward thrust begins, is not to
say it must occur from the 'top' of the foot movement, by virtue of these variations (and it is with
respect to them especially that problems of 'data
reduction' are presented in watching a body pulsing). But it must occur along with the onset of the
accelerational thrust, at point A above, for example, or destinational coincidence cannot be
smoothly achieved.

When I articulate a course of notes and must
strike the final one of the sequence in conjunction
with the next beating, articulations are distributed
through the course of a movement preceding a
final accelerational thrust. The pace of a course of
beat-oriented articulations is orderly with respect
to phases of an undulating movement.

A sequential course of articulations is paced in
a certain fashion, and is paced by reference to a
prospective time of arrival at the completion of a
phase. In a recurrent pulsing situation, as in music,

a phase is organized as a stable accomplishment; but whether a stable pulse is detectable or not, all reaches are given their smoothness and internal pacing layouts by reference to prospectivities of arrival time, even when a 'shifting pulse,' better, shifting prospectivities, are accomplished. When I say 'word,' I stretch forward to the end of the production, establishing an orderly flow in the course of the production that will bring me toward its completion at a preknown time, and the internal durational spacings of the course of movements that 'word' is are molded by the temporal prospectivity of the course.

Say five notes are to be played, the fifth occurring in conjunction with a beating. A pace must be chosen for these notes, and when I begin to play, a pace is chosen for the second note relative to the first, as soon as I begin. And this pace, in turn, is itself chosen by reference to the end of the phase of movements and their spatial array for the hand. In jazz play, when I start a sequence of notes with a certain pacing, I commit myself to a number of notes to be executed until some prospective arrival node. If I am to play six notes, or seven, three, or twelve, a pacing is established for the reach, is determined at the outset with a pace set in the opening two, and is internally modifiable only in an orderly fashion. If the first two notes are set for a six-noted passage, I may not set out fast and then slow down within the course of a phase toward a 'termination time' and reach destinational coincidence. A course of speeded movement is undertaken that *implies* a number of notes to follow and implicates a manner of forward movement for the hand, a manner of movement that must be brought to the necessary sort of completion if the gesture is to proceed smoothly, without faltering or tripping.

There are various qualifications here. For example, I may begin very rapidly and allow a pausing prior to reaching for a final note in conjunction with the beat. But even if a break of this

sort should occur, a course of notes between one |
tap and the next therefore not equidistant, the first
notes will be articulationally aimed toward the
'top' of the upbeat phases, a virtual standing-still of
the foot tapping, for example, will constitute a
pausing in the succession, and then a final reaching may be made. A reach forward on the downstroke may be bypassed altogether, however, the
upswing phase providing the prospective 'segment,' and a next course then taken in an orderly
fashion with respect to a 'later' cycle. And further
shiftings and 'expansions' of the accentual structur-
ing, organized over a moving course of action, are
sustainable, a fact of central significance for extended articulations.

Returning to my jazz development, I came to
learn to reach with pacings prospective to 'expanding' and 'contracting' arrival times, stretched
toward when the soundful availability of that
number of entailed notes, lying in thus and such a
distanced array for the hand, had been properly
assessed by the hand's appraisals of the terrain and
its own articulational capacities in it. Such accomplishments will be described shortly.

III

Every once in a while the time would get into
the fingers as I sat and tried to move like Jimmy
Rowles, setting a beat first by getting my shoulders going around a little, while I tapped my foot
and snapped my fingers before play; counting off
the time with a care I had never taken before, a
care for the jazz to be played, a care for the others
with whom I would have been coordinating my
moves, for that bass player and drummer who were
never around, that we might stride into the song
together; a care for the new listener I had become
myself and for the one who had been missing,
ready to hear that song, that jazz, to tap his fingers
to it.

Taking the role of the other with this caretaking beat, every once in a while, so it at first seemed, the time would get into the fingers. One of the ways I would try to keep it there was to stay in a place for a while, playing the same few notes over and over again, thrusting moves gaining an ever more solid and stable shape, saying this same thing again and again and again, so that all of me might stride into the song together. And the song was already under way, the improvised jazz song, with a handful of notes said again and again and again and then again a slight bit differently, expanding matters somewhat and getting the time into the hands more thoroughly, gaining a nice grasp of the place, a good jazz tonicity and mobility for the hand established, the hand well thrusting and gaining a strong sense of its numerical capabilities and placement. It has so many digits, there is so much to the terrain, there is so fast or slow to go, so far, singing a song as I go along, and the hand had to gain a strong sense of its numerical capabilities, the numbers of the places and the fingerness of the organ, as the typist who digs in for an unfamiliar sight becomes especially 'attentive' to the fingerness of the hands and the field of action.

Taking first breaths between phrases, getting the time into the fingers and shoulders, my hand would often 'find itself' positioned on the keyboard in such a posture:

just before entering a passage of play. Were you to watch or view a film of the jazz pianist's hands, you would see poised stances frequently assumed prior to a noted part of the musical action. So this photo could be well taken (though it was not) during ongoing play at a rather slow shutter speed with little blur. So too could one like this:

and during the course of the carriage's return I posturally ready myself at times to pick up again with a thought in its midst. And here a 'word' may be known in advance of my renewed entrance into the terrain, as a handful readiness while I almost say the word but never quite do so, pursing my lips to say it as I purse my fingers to do it, holding onto the thought during this breath, never saying it until it shall be articulationally said with sequential movements as a soundful sighting.

Or a word's beginning may be handfully anticipated, a beginning whose opening movements will receive proper gestural development and consequent looks here. The articulational reaching goes toward and through places along essentialized and ever-present paced ways of terrain traverse. These define the movement modalities of finger talking, making, for example, 'ed' or 'ing' or 'ily' or 'ful' or 's' place achievements sensibly part of the unfolding course of movements; the improvisational hands have ways of traverse for negotiatively paying off on commitments to do good-looking sayables through and through.

The improvisatory jazz hand, alive to ranges of possibilities in its essentialized grasp of good ways always present, may hover over such places as the piano places shown above, tasting possibilities here and there, doing the jazz that way. Having to keep the action under way, long pauses for reflection never very judicious in jazz, music gets improvisationally made out of movements exploratorily akin to the alternating back and forth between *shift* keys I may here do: as I pause for reflection in the course of finger talking, bouncing back and forth with the little fingers from one shift key to another; 'allowing' the other hand to reflect in its hoverings for a good next move to get the wayful reaching ready again; feeling a *This* or a *Here* or an *As* to open the sentence; finding in such bouncing back and forth that a ready reach may be exploratorily come upon, without prefiguring apart from these hoverings at times, as the basketball player dribbles the ball first with this hand then that, searching for an opening in the line of defense and a course for setting off into the running action.

Such explorations as the typing writer may undertake are inaccessible in the sights here of course, the work of writing not recoverable from them, the activities of much writing not requiring, at least, that the action be kept under way that way, though often critically involving them. *Shift* key work is not a publicized part of writing, as a course of singly stated notes bounced back and forth between two digits, as the improvisatory hand finds itself situated on a good way to move at a certain pace into a longer reach, are of the jazz finger sayings for others. Actions there take on many qualities that keeping sayings under way entails.

Now finding myself taking breaths between phrases, emulating Jimmy Rowles's shoulder breathing, the hand would find itself situated in such poised positions. I began to tell it to linger, tasting possibilities, to find ways of traverse singingly available, essentialized ways of routing right there at hand: known to be at hand right there as routes for thus and such a pacing course, as 'routes quickly traversable when at hand this way there,' as routes not usable without venturing when at hand this way there. Staying on a way at all times, remaining singingly present with the fingers, the ways began to become expressly appreciated, with hands instructably guided to them as: *terrain courses at hand here and there for classes of pacing possibilities.*

With the hand poised over a passage of notes, a particular digit ready over a particular key, a good deal of melodying was soundfully possible, going up and then down quickly over this course. The hand was able to take an array of notes beneath it with pacing moves from left to right or right to left, or one way then the other then the other, for example, with a rocking course quickly paced up to an ahead toward which the mobile hand was aimed, reaching for a good-sounding place, for good-sounding yet not prefigured places ahead. A safe way was had for knowing what the next notes sounded like, through multiple repetitions over the same places, the first times through establishing 'sounds for gearing in with the fingers,' these not quite 'sounds of melodies at hand.'* A way was had to stay singingly on that route for so many noted sayings without venturing, not a way to be overly used, a way among many for appraising the whereabouts and fingerness and pace-able presence of ways, such appraisings making up this 'strategically' accomplished music at the same time. Ways for these hands' new looks, familiar sounds, and tactilely appreciated caretaking be-

*See the note on p. 149.

came strategically instructable as I began to find my fingers singing that jazz.

Taking a breath between phrases, I began to assume such safe stances as emulating Jimmy Rowle's means of setting a tempo gave me pause for thought. I discovered the jazz happening in the looks of the hands and familiar sounds of the music in ways I began to use such safe stances frequently, at first too frequently for they were so productive.

Moving from such a handfull of notes:

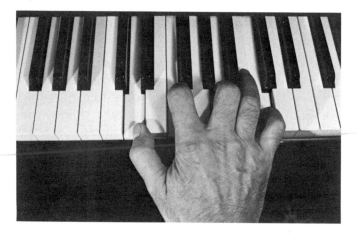

onto a diminished path, for example:

from one chord specific, characteristic jazz-sounding route to another (say in the context of a G

minor-C dominant chord change, a common progression type), such safe stancing after shoulder
breathing began to afford handful means for interchordal melodying as a continuous accomplishment. Examination of this switch, characteristic of
many such maneuvers, can serve as a productive
example.

Moving from chord to chord I would, for instance, undertake a course aimed toward a next
downbeat for the second chord. The left hand
grabs a first chord, a first textured-sounding constellation of places, and then reaches toward the
next, a C dominant. An articulational reaching tra-
verses these paths, from the 'G way,' we may say,
onto this 'C way,' speaking nonmusicologically but
handfully now:

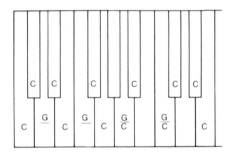

The chord progression would be given sounding presence by an interweaving course of melodying that jazzfully realized its implications, as
implications obtaining between 'parts' of the jazz
body. The chordal hand would reconfigurate continuously, its shapings undergoing a smooth modification. This finger has to spread farther for the
next stance than that, this finger moves faster,
spreading farther apart so that arrival at the next
destination is achieved, as noted in my introduction to the chord, with the hand coming into position for the grab ready to do it just then. These 'fingers,' this chordal hand, underwent fine internal
modifications along all dimensions, inside and out,
with a pacing structure of molding movement that
can be viewed as articulatory in its own right. This

paced ('dot-connecting') reaching, to the new place it knows so well, as the cupped hand knows the chin, the caller's reach knows the shape of the receiver—these molded articulations were finely organized by the accentual thrust that its placement, as this beat, will announce. The progression is soundfully melodied now, as a textured saying said just then, each distance achievement of the molding reach paced to bring about the just-there-then-ness of the chord production.

And I would tell myself quite explicitly, noticing the jazz-ness in the hand's looks and familiar sounds with such an at first incidental happening, to use such safe stances as were adopted as jumping-off springboards. I started into a left to right, or right to left, or mixed reaching, with a rocking movement over these 'four places' beneath the hand on the G way. And I stretched toward a next accent that could be come down upon after a high lift-off, the hand finding a way, through such rocking, to disengage and get off the keyboard before a downthrust. I would find myself able to aim toward the C way in ways that would assure its rapidly traversable availability there. I began to use such springboard actions for doing path switch-ings.

Going from left to right, taking four notes for example, my hand would follow an arc, so that were I to draw a line aimed toward a next 'dot,' a line drawn as though tracing the shape of the course of articulations, a pacing like this would be portrayed:

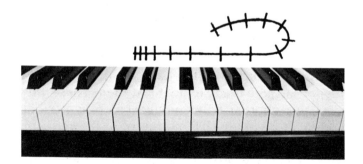

In just lifting off the keyboard, I would find myself coming back down into the terrain, to get into the diminished scale, in a way my hands had this diminished scale available for rapid traverse. It was not that I could not take a course like this:

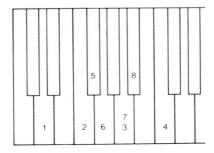

without a high lift-off to get into configurational shape for the diminished way available for rapid traverse. It was that in just lifting off, getting an undulating time into the fingers, I then found myself able to do a path-switching maneuver in ways I had previously never attempted. A means to get from way to way began to show itself, I learned from it, and began doing springboarding as an instructable maneuver.

How is this diminished way, the C way, a way available for rapid traverse? The rapid way I had this routing available involved a fingering solution long ago worked out as the way to finger this scale for up-and-down fastness. This solution for the way fastly done involved these assignments:

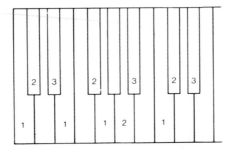

Going up the four-noted course, aimed toward a next beat in the reach for a next note as the chordal grab arrived at its destination, a synchrony of place achievements with continuous ready-set-goes in the hand, shoulders, everywhere, and lifting high off the keyboard, there was that C way approachable with the second finger on the F#, to give one example among many possibilities. Aiming for this way, aiming for a 'melody beginning' that would begin on this way, getting that second finger onto the F# was to get on the path in ways I had it available for rapid traverse. This is not to say I cannot play this scale with other fingers, for I later learned to construct an articulational move with a pacing manner that enabled much in-course digital reorganization. But I had it firmly available as a C way for rapid upward or downward travel with the second finger on the F#, and coming up high after a lift-off, without venturing, without lunging, I found a new way of having room to align the hand to start a fast word beginning.

The hand rose with a high lift-off; the upward course of four notes began after the G minor chord had been stated, as the chordal hand was already on its way toward the statement of the next beat as the landing on the C dominant chord; the foot rose up after the tap, and a slight configurational alignment was smoothly occurring during the silent music above the keyboard. The melodic hand would come down into the C way like this:

ready for entrance on the way for an upward course, a melody beginning poised for before the engagement, an articulational course into a way with an almost chordal stance.

Aiming for a course of articulation toward a beat the next chord was 'part of,' being interchordal now this way, the hand took room to breathe in the arm and shoulder's undulations in synchrony with the left hand's reach and foot's participations. And getting somewhat high off the keyboard at first became part of an articulational unfolding that would have the C way coming into reach through the course of the turnaround and downward accelerational thrust. The C way would be poised for, as in a melody-beginning configuration with the F# and turned-under thumb, prepared for as a C way for continued upward melodying.

Or the C way could be much more essentially and latently part of the breathing configuration. I can come at this routing with a single pointed finger and still be wayfully aimed in my articulational moves. I can play the diminished scale (in our example) thusly up and down, knowing its distances so that the multifarious routings from here to there upon it are manageable achievements that the arm and shoulders may 'compensatorily' participate in, up above and back from the single pointed finger. But I do not have this way as a quickly available way to make long scalar melodies, for example, without my familiar handful engagement on that route, pacingly traversed as a handful of many notes.

The melodic reach back down into the terrain for the C way quickly available from this F#, among my first new interchordal accomplishments, would then move rapidly up this way but might fall into difficulties as a next chord was being grabbed. Broader nodes for accentual targeting were not well set as a time in the hands, shoulders, everywhere. And at first I would, getting springboardingly on the C way had there, often proceed quickly up the keyboard—not with that knowing where you are going continuously modifiable over the course, with a small strip of targetable places moving right along just up ahead of unfoldingly prefiguring sequentialized reaches. I would instead proceed with an unsinging continuation, the C path's layout given as a long layout, by reaching ways that would often get to some 'any notes thereabout' as the next chord came up. And I would fall out of singing touch with the hands in falling off a wayful aim toward still a next chord-ally wayful routing, out of gear with a specifically paced saying said just now and then, the jazz would fade from control on this fragile precipice, the temporal-spatial synchrony of my singings broken, the rest of the passage not that interweaving jazz on the records.

Taking breaths, starting 'late' into a course of such handfully available, rockingly swift moves over notes digitally present, after the left-hand stretch had already settled into its now sounding, melodied place; swiftly pacing a move through such at-fingertip notes toward a firm prospective accentual landing, able to rock up and down or doubly over such a handful; doing manifold possibilities with a digitally anchored passage aimed toward that firm prospectivity; finding I could move from familiar way to familiar way, a security of aim experienced in that very fact, the jazz seen and heard in it as well; a singability enabled, at least, in being thoroughgoingly wayful—finding this I did springboarding in many ways, as here:

passage, for instance, in a pacingly smooth move up to a new sector, I was prospectively aligned toward the C way a bit higher up, without thumb turn-unders for smooth interchordal transitions.

And the hand could configurationally shape toward the C way come upon in this fashion with new latitudes for routings, with a deeper improvisationality present in the ways of its prospective movement toward a variously handleable array. Springboarding to a higher register, I 'found myself' configurationally prospective down to the C way not for only either upward-or-downward movement.

Coming upon the C way from above, moving down toward this little bunching of good-sounding places, moving from one unfolding posturing to another through the springboarding arc, I would take it as a bunching for manifold directed courses. Present for the hand, not now just as the C way to go long ways with, but as a segment of the C way to go multiple short ways with, in the very fact of this after-the-beat sector jump I would begin to employ such a way come upon as a ready-at-hand cluster for varied articulational use.

Not doing lunging now but smooth springboarding, I would find myself moving wayfully from poised stance to poised stance, sequentially unfolding on the way down toward the little bunching. I would find on the way down, as a finding smoothly made on the way down, as a sequential readiness pacingly molded toward that arrival time, which one of a number of directions and ratings to employ as a noted saying. I would find what to say, with a hand coming onto a way singingly from a way, definite targetability coming right up beneath it. The hand unfolded from the peak of the turnaround toward this sequentialized preparation:

for a little up, or up-then-down, or up-then-down-then-up course, or this way:

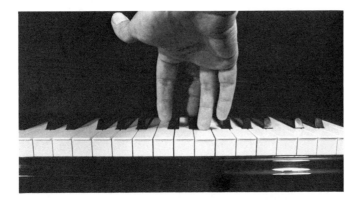

for interdigitating possibilities I had formerly seldom employed in my pathway practicing. And a more familiar jazz ordering began to be seen and heard here, as my instructions to do springboarding, do interweaving, change directions frequently, change paces frequently, took notice of first happenstance orderings, and employably instituted them, each interacting with the other in my conversation from above.

Getting the time into the fingers and hand, coming down for a saying to be said just so, having a soundful way right at hand in these first rather cautious yet increasingly smooth sector shifts, I began to find, in the undulating nature of my entrance and pacingly tuned interdigitations, that I could undertake new sorts of shaped and rated courses with well-at-hand route segments. While the C way in such a sector-shifting jump was at first come upon still as that C way for rapid traverse, as a segment of the way quickly known for the hand digitally ready for its notes, a range of new ways of moving and assessing and pacing and fingering began to emerge.

Moving now from way to way without extensively long stretches always in hand, the hand would sequentially come into the way with unfolding realization of the stance. This stance might entail the hand over the new sector like this:

with the little finger prospectively target*able* toward the F#. The little finger is now part of a handful engagement with the C way non-lungefully present, and not just for long scalar melodying. Taking breaths, letting time go by, considerable posturing took place at first, ways became reconstituted as right there at hand, and I would come upon this C way right there at hand with a prospectively shaping stance ill suited for a long upward rapidity, for example, but well suited for an opening anchored negotiation.

Doing after-the-beat springboarding toward the C way's places this way, with a little finger coming toward a place in the unfolding encounter that had not been a place for it before: routes were becoming freshly appreciated with new digital placement possibilities, new directional possibilities, the time in the hands to permit pacings through ways with digital placements appropriate for such fingerings. The hand learned more about fingering-pacing relations.

My hand already knew the ways not merely as spatial affairs for its essentializations, but as ways for the digits relative to particular note assignments for classes of action. So that the C way under consideration would not be scalefully ascended, farther up the line with a little finger on the F#, at least not for a rapid and evenly paced course involving a turn-under of the thumb beneath that finger—into the G, A, and Bb of the C way for a scalar rise—not without appropriate 'prior measures.'

I would come down into the terrain with prospective sequentialized decision. Starting with a pace entailing so many further notes, I would, for example, go quickly up the course of the way to the F# and then quickly back down. The hand would find the availability of the way present for such a maneuver and find, through the course of a quick rise, the generation of a commitment to a mode of traverse to involve *that* F# or not. If so, it was involved as the upward boundary of a course, at least a first time through. A first time through, at least, because on a second time through I could either do that turn-under as was customary for continued upward travel, getting the thumb down on the preceding note so as to bring the second finger to the F#. Or, most significant among my new discoveries, I would do a turn-under beneath this new F#. The hand could now appraise, in a first pass, how that scale could be taken in this new way, a sharpening of precise digitational acuity gained through an exploratory pass, a securing of the places attainable that way, with the time in the fingers, with a strong prospectivity from early into the ascent for a longer under-reaching thumb stretch to get the hand beneath the little finger just there then.

And to start with a pace entailing so many notes that whether or not to use *this* F# could be decided in and through the course of a quick rise, and not configurationally in advance of its sequentialized approach, involved a knowing of the paceable presence of the ways with a hand whose digital numericity was most essentially being appreciated.

It was not that a layout in advance was required for digital counting. It was that the hand was on a way where an *order* of fastness could be managed knowingly. It was that the hand knew its ways, with these ways, so that, for example, entering this diminished C way bunching with such a digitally configurated unfolding, going *up or down* could be done within a known range of rapidity. Going with *alternating,* rather than left-to-right digitations, could be done within some other, perhaps partially overlapping, range. But in the second practice, as one instance, going like this:

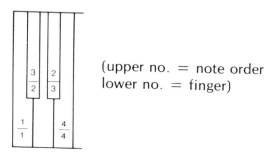

(upper no. = note order
lower no. = finger)

the hand knew the bunching so as to know that such alternating passage could not be prospective toward places farther up the C way *that* way, not without appropriate prior measures.

The C way known that way, for alternational digiting, was known so that such actions would be kept bounded before doing alternational venturing away from the bunch without a pacing shift, without reconfigurational breathing. And it would be bounded in this instance to the bunch itself. This array was known pacingly for alternating digitations that could be rapidly sustained this way:

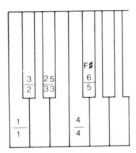

or with multiple repetitions of alternating moves, as one possibility.

This knowing of the pace-able presence of ways was by now a generalized knowing, for the hand had the terrain everywhere known for pace-abilities, relative to its acquisitions. Being over any 'bunching' was to be in a known range of pace-ability for rocking moves back and forth; being spread over a 'handful' was to be in a pace-able range for rocking moves, and also for 'howsoever' pace-able actions of a large number of classes. There were outer-inner rockings, or rockings with repetitions for part of the way always extendable in continuous pace into a rocking over all or more of it, to give two 'class' examples among many.

To so know the ways was to be temporally there so as to afford an unfolding prospectivity to appraisings of numericity. A rapidly paced entry into a way thusly known could have it with sure availability for articulational commitment without a prefiguring digital counting. Its essentialized pace-able presence in this sense afforded securely paced entries, whose soundfully targeted particu-

lar places would be found in course, doing improvisation.

This essentialized pace-able presence was
generalized to globally involve an appreciation for
classes of handful presences in the keyboard: to a
spread hand, to a bunched hand, a poised and
digitally note-targeted hand, a hand doing rapid
scale ascensions, a hand doing arpeggiated turn-
unders. But the note specificity of *a* particular
array or a particular sequentially unfolding traverse
interactively participated with this generalized
appreciation. I cannot do *any* arpeggiation with
any particular degree of fastness. The extensiveness of a prospectively committed pacing always
takes the particular ways into caretaking account.
The generalized appreciation with which I can
come assuredly 'fast' into any 'bunching,' for example, knowing I can play fast in such quarters,
finds the engagement with some particular jazz-
making bunch always particularly consequential.
Though I can alternationally digitate in familiar
jazz-paced ways on my tabletop, at the piano *that
C way* bunchingly just there in particular, for instance, poses unfoldingly revealed requirements
specific to its configurationally unique digitalize-
able contours.

And appropriate prior measures, like a shoulder breathing, afforded a precise digitational
acuity to be formed, getting the time into the
hands. . . . It afforded a movement into a course
that, with a shift in a means of approach, a toning
up of the hand's destinational presence to a precisely shaped sector of the terrain, could now be
taken with a manner of continued alternating digi-
tation up the line. It afforded an ascent that in
former un-breathing play might have been attempted in the new sector and trippingly realized.
The time would have to be solidly in the shoulders,
hands, fingers, arm, everywhere, for such acuities
to be gained in maneuvers as with the little-finger-
ed F# turn-under, after an exploratory first pass:

Such practices as first pass assessing, and even the explicit use of 'wrong fingers,' became instructably undertaken at first, maximizing now, it might be said, not the most efficacious way to move fast but the most jazzful way to be at the piano, the music's looks and sounds seen and heard as instigations and payoffs.

But using 'wrong fingers,' and doing repeated passes so as to do 'finger-solution jazz,' initially productive as express practices, were only most preliminarily so formulated in play as express practices, by reference to the historical context of their relevant emergence, regarded and undertaken this way against the background of 'correctly fingered paths.' So too would I come to instruct myself to do fingering changes as a mobile practice in its own right, as here:

where going up the G way I would pace toward the Bb of the C way with the fourth finger, aiming for it as a next accentual landing. I would aim there and hold there as a place to land, coming down into the C way at times quite intentionally to afford an 'opportunity' for a finger change. Bouncing off the Bb and setting back down into it with the middle finger, with a pacing fastly aimed downward toward a time of arrival farther up ahead, I was quickly aimed along the way, now a secure and many-noted route when entered on the rebound. And while, in my earlier play, finger changes arose on occasions of trouble, they now began to arise as of the music, holding on to a soundful way by staying soundful, rather than trying to pick up the pieces of an already disintegrating saying.

I began to do fingering changes with increasing improvisational intent, using 'wrong fingers' and 'struggling fingers' from the standpoint, for example, of the way a very competent sight reader at the piano does fingering, and 'right fingerings' that often indeed appear quite bizarre from the classicist's perspective—right jazz fingerings. The competent sight reader, having to take a long passage, foresees that passage with a looking at the score that is as finely integrated with the movements of his fingers as is the looking of the competent text-reproducing typist. Foreseeing it 'that way,' having to foresee it that way to do that work, an often strong constraint in live sight reading, foreseeing its fingerability, he will seldom if ever find himself in a situation he might be occupationally disposed to see my hands as 'finding themselves in.'

For I would instructionally undertake finger changes not for the express sake of realigning my way onto a route particularly prospective beneath an entering reach—with a sense for the path as a whole present in such motivated realignments—but would undertake such changes as would appear to amount to nothing.

Though they would appear to amount to nothing, a generalized improvisational mobility was amounting to that jazz on the records. Staying in a particular sector, the time well into the fingers, hands, shoulders, everywhere, shifting on the same note from the fourth finger to the second, posturing upwardly, then back on the same note extending downwardly, then doing the saying midhandedly, now I would go into a multiplaced course handfully begun with that finger I had originally employed for a same starting place.

In such dancing about, extending downwardly or upwardly, my hand was not feeling its way about in the dark, not spreading out to gain contact with the terrain to assess a way's pace-able athandness by taking an anticipatorily explicit spatial stock, touching a particular way for example. My hand was now in fact extending upwardly or downwardly as here:

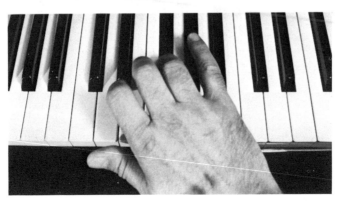

and while a new preparatory stance was often assumed during fingering shifts, the wayfulness of the terrain as a place for jazz singing was being everywhere taken into continuously thematic account by a continuously jazzful organ: spreading out for an unfoldingly explicit commitment to a fast saying, shifting essentialized fulcrums of extensions as a very jazzful was to do sparse sayings, singing with the fingers.

Two-chord inter-melodying was occurring through such practices as springboardings and finger changes, for example, but that jazz on the records was spoken in sentences, and a longer reaching was required. Many of my short phrases were now well formed in being pacingly well placed, and new orders of paced-placing began to emerge as these well-said phrase and sentence fragments became part of adult jazz sayings.

As I began doing breathings, getting off the keyboard and down into a run in configurationally pace-assessing shape for a further move up, I would at first come into the switched-onto path with a strong accentual thrust, pacing an articulation over such a handful as examined above, aimed toward a time of arrival up ahead coincident with the hand-grabbing chord reach, coincident with its participation in the very next beat.

Coming down on this F# with the second finger:

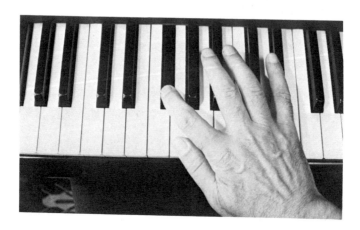

I came down with an accelerating rapidity, striking it hard, doing the very next beat as an assertive just-then-ness opening.

The aim of the articulational reach proceeded in concert with the aim of the chordal reaching toward a strong downthrust in common, as the foot struck the floor 'on' that next beat, and a more solidly 'systemic' synchrony between left-hand reachings and right-hand articulational aims was being gained through my emulations of Jimmy Rowles's shoulder breathing. And such prospectively synchronous reachings became increasingly expansive in scope, for as I would reach into a familiar routing had at hand for a long stretch, finding its availability at hand for a long stretch in ways indicated, I could often come now to set out fast up the line in new ways.

In my beginning discoveries of springboarding, with the instigations and payoffs of these looks and sounds, I set out for a long stretch on that familiarly fast C-diminished way, to continue with this example, often at first setting out fast without respect for where that would bring me. But as the establishment of a stably thrusting beating became an increasingly consistent mode of mobile presence at the keyboard, all my melodying practices began to come under the jurisdiction of opportunities for wayful and synchronous negotiation that it facilitated. This beat becoming the ways of the arms and shoulders, its stable accentualities and de-accentualities of cyclical thrusting afforded an increasingly fluid in-course prospectivity molding in my articulational moves. The use of a way for rapid traverse, the use of all ways, negotiatively proceeding through the course of an improvisational singing with the fingers, now happened like this:

The left hand would reach from chord to chord, and the right would sequentially traverse the terrain, and a course of continuously firm rotational moves was 'defining' the beats, and subdividingly defining the beats, and expansively defining the beats. For as an articulational course was being taken up or down, interweavingly through the keyboard, entry into the terrain, shiftings of pacings of noted work in the terrain, disengagements from the terrain, refingerings and reconfigurings in the terrain, springboardings in the terrain, moving up a line beat by beat and then breaking into a multi-note-per-beat flurry through the terrain — such pacings off the tips of the fingers' thrusting could proceed in the following ways.

The articulational course could now take up in downbeat synchrony with the foot; now in upbeat synchrony with the left hand's rise toward a next chord; now in top-of-the-turnaround synchrony within the one-shoulder-sway-per-four-foot bounces; now jumping in on the upbeat phase of a chordal reaching arc and taking a soundful traverse through thus and so many places to a foot downbeat, one that was 'located within' the course of the broader reaching arc of the chordal stretch; now extending fast from 'within' the chordal reach to a farther upahead downbeat, simultaneously making contact with some good note as the chord grasp 'finally' reached the goal it would reposingly pass through; now reaching out for a fast run through a course of ways aimed toward a periodically modifiable series of accentual landmarks, prospective periodicities of and for jazz hands' pace-ably wayful sayings, which would traverse the duration of multi-landmarking left-hand reachings.

A reach over the duration of several left-hand unfoldings was interweavingly now of an accentual patterning that involved the chordal reaches themselves. This chord was passed through with accelerational deemphasis, the right hand stretching farther ahead around the bend of a turnaround, or through an attenuating intonational ascent or descent; the next punctuated in synchrony with a strong melodic landing; and with this chordal articulating of a slow melody down there, said just now and just then, just this hard and this soft,

right-hand reachings were interweavingly giving
jazz presence to a progression of landmarkings
through places traversed since the sixteenth cen-
tury.

As the left hand would pass over a chord, the
melodying hand would, for example, making its
in-course appraisals, slow down slightly as it did a
little springboarding turnaround that was hardly a
divingboard sort of operation, but rather a little
puddle-jumping-Gene Kelly-"Singing in the Rain"
step. And springboarding of the sort described
above can be consulted as indicating mobilities
and appraisings that were thoroughgoingly present
in continuously in-course accentual modifications
within the span of a broader shoulder breathing
that first was instigated by and paid off on with
jazzful high-jumpings.

IV

As the time got into the fingers, hands, arms,
shoulders, everywhere, altogether new relationships between chords and paths were being ful-
filled now, the analytic character of my note
choices, as good notes for such chords, coming
under consistently thoroughgoing reformulation as
a handful choosing, the song as a progression of
demarcated and harmonically conceived placements becoming a rather different formatting
structure.

For now I would do jazz sayings that increasingly brought my full 'vocabular' resources, my
full range of wayful reachings, into the service of
that jazz on the records, into the hands' ways of
pace-ably traversing not from route to route, but
doing singings. And the language of paths and path
switchings, born of my instructed introduction to
jazz music and deeply intrinsic to the nature of my
selectional negotiations for so long, thoroughly
situated in the image-guided traverse ways of my
past, must be abandoned.

Standing outside my play and looking down at

my hands, searching for paths to identify as I had
over my teacher's shoulder years before, one could
speak of my new modes of traverse by identifying
'note orderings' in such terms, watching a moment's play:

Coming up a diminished path for four successive notes,
he switches into a three-note chromatic turnaround, and then
up in fourths three intervallic steps, down into a major triad
that accords well with the next chord about to be played, and
passing through this triad as the next chord is already an-
nounced, he arpeggiates up and then down a seven-note
course of minor-sixth intervals; taking a quick major triad that
would not accord well with this chord in Bach, but accords
well with this chord since Beethoven, he proceeds over this
dissonant path into a resolution by landing on the third of a
next major chord on its second beat in the measure, and with
a next chord he plays a dissonant scale starting on the major
second degree relative to the chord, which goes up the keyboard in stepwise fashion and then doubles back over that
scale, going down it in fourths . . .

Had I filmed and slowed down my teacher's
play so that such identifications could be made, so
that those mysterious interweavings could be 'reduced' to such ways of talking, to an enumeration
of nameable places and nameable devices producing these 'characteristic jazz sounds,' I probably
would have given up right then and there. Encountering problems of nomenclature and 'intricacies of
structure' that would have made practicing the
piano impossible, was I now to practice a 'diminished scale' or practice a 'diminished scale followed by or interspersed with chromatic half
steps'; should I call it a 'diminished scale' in the
first place, or search the looks with ways of looking
that would yield broader classificatory principles;
should that movement down in fourths be generally practiced or should it be a movement down in
fourths along certain particular paths; and what
path *was* the 'movement down in fourths' a movement along, for multiple paths could be said to be
fourthingly traversed; or should I find an alterna-
tive 'background' route being alternatingly tra-

versed, assuming there was one as I did, which
would then make it not down in fourths but, for
instance, 'down the suspended dominant chord on
X degree of the new route'?

When he extracted a piece of melody under
my urgings, to speak of its construction, he was affording me a text of practices, ways of speaking I
could carry around in my head, my imaginings, my
looks, my fingers' ways, a phrase book of pictured
'melodies.' And saying 'you can use a diminished
scale here,' extracting a nameable route to formulate his doings for 'my' sake, he gave me a way to
formulate mine each day at the piano. And it
worked to get me started, started on the route toward ways he did not tell me about. Having that
path, having its insufficiency continually leading
me to do more with it, having that record collection, it worked to sustain daily practicings, allocate
my time at the keyboard, find this and that to practice in particular, find progress taking place. And
through improvisationally motivated practicings
with a sizable corpus of such routes, I gained essentialized handful command awaiting syntactic
synthesis through jazz temporalizations.

Were it not for the development of interests to
write an account of my progress, I would probably
now say, as he felt obliged to urge at the same time
as he was obliged to teach: I don't think about
where I am going, I make it up as I go along. Had
he more explicitly urged me to 'get the phrasing
right,' or had I been more inclined and perhaps occupationally compelled to learn by first getting
some simple sentences together, a different course
of socialization might have evolved.*

*One does not have to learn about places by their names
to become an improvisor, though most beginners do much of
this these days, and most recent jazz vocabulary shows it.
Wayful proceedings are taken that often bespeak their origins
in practicings along the sorts of routes that have been 'heavily
influenced' by the recent written tradition. To speak colloquially, you must practice your scales; learners these days write
down pictures to aid that, elaborate these pictures and produce new scales telling of conversations between musicians,

A vocabulary was provided and spoken of in terms of note-to-chord relations, as I was taught a way to learn to speak song-formatted jazz. A host of paths were elaborated in terms of theoretic formulations of such note-to-chord relations, and practicings along these paths yielded a repertoire of chord-specific ways. Paths were elaborated in terms that were not conceived as chord-specific from a nomenclatural standpoint. A 'chromatic path,' an array of 'intervals of a fourth,' of 'alternating half steps and minor third steps,' of 'up a whole step down two whole steps'—to name some instances of class examples in such terms—such non-chord-specific-so-to-speak paths were elaborated. Practicing along these paths yielded a repertoire of wayful, securely targettable, essentialized modalities of place-achieving aims with routes so conceived.

But I had come to learn that the problem of note selection and note orderings was a problem of my history, with these lessons, and this talk about music, with these routes, with these aimed-for records, these instances of jazz toward which I aspired.

The notion of a melody, too, formulated above as a doing something with something down before, with such practices as repetitions, inversions, and essential repetitions, descriptive of my

---

jazz players with classical training, years working over named keyboards.

The inference here is, however, never unambiguous. The most complex possibilities are not inconceivably attained by listening to records and doing no theorizing. But in modern literate circles, where a language undergoes continuous and substantial modification over single generational careers, where playing fast and intricately has come to competitively differentiate performers in a scarce marketplace, where being a good musician means to be multilingual—in such a set of circumstances, speaking colloquial sociology, the days of that young man and his horn, sitting every night on the edge of the bandstand, practicing every day, learning to speak jazz like one first learns to speak a first language, are poverty-stricken and numbered.

ways of being musical at that point, can, standing
outside of the production and reflecting upon such
a matter, be appropriately reconsidered.

For now a repetitional intent, for example,
sustained, as a generalized caretaking throughout
play, to do things with things formerly done in
having consistently jazzful hands, is 'manifest' in
such practices as staying in a territory for a while,
being jazzfully caretaking by lingering, establishing a strong wayful point of departure for further
venturings, doing such 'strategic melodying,' doing
jazz competently. And staying in a territory I play
the 'same notes' again on occasion, and repetitions
may be said to be sustained. But I play them wayfully and in appropriately paced ways at all times,
and any express repetitional intent that should
emerge during the course of play (and I may at
times nudge myself to do that one again) is realized in and through the course of jazzing handful
play.

So, for example, a repetition will take on its
forms by reference to the improvisational ways indicated above. If it repeats only essential features
of the preceding, looking at matters from without,
it is not a failing repetition, but a repetition singingly done that way. If it strictly duplicates the preceding, looking at the 'one piece of melody' and
the 'next,' freezing the segments for comparative
study either through a rendering procedure such as
a text affords, or in that sort of 'listening' which
may be comparatively motivated—if 'it' duplicates
a preceding 'fragment,' the melodicality *is* hands
lingering-there ways.

When a 'repetition' can be said to occur, there
are now such incidences as: a little fragment repeated at twice its original speed followed by another fragment of a preceding figure played at
one-third its former rate; a melody fragment repeated much more rapidly than the preceding as a
way into a longer course of reachings; a melody
fragment inserted into a longer passage that repeats a portion of some preceding figure; a melody

fragment turned upside-down, said twice as fast, leading into another fragment that says what was said long before, at half speed, in alternating steps rather than sequentially precise restatement. And this list can go on as endlessly as can a terminology of paths, presents exactly the same 'problems' of nomenclature, defines units in exactly the same ways as units for analysis, and in fact is an artifice of conceptual rather than productional ways of talking about melody.

For there is no melody, there is melodying. And melodying practices are handful practices as soundfully aimed articulational reaching. There is no end to ways for characterizing the 'structure of a melody,' given the possibilities of terminological revision, theoretic reclassification and structural analysis. But the action essentially escapes descriptive attention. If it can be said that I 'do repetitions,' it must then be asked: how do jazz hands behave so as to produce 'appearances' for a material examination by all the talk about them.

I learned this language through five years of overhearing it spoken. I had come to learn, overhearing and overseeing this jazz as my instructable hands' ways—in a terrain nexus of hands and keyboard whose respective surfaces had become known as the respective surfaces of my tongue and teeth and palate are known to each other—that this jazz music is ways of moving from place to place as singings with my fingers. To define jazz (as to define any phenomenon of human action) is to describe the body's ways.

Little bits and pieces of jazz-handlings showed themselves to me, revealed as that jazz music in my hands' ways, and I did nudgings to myself, taking an inner course of action to help the outer one out, it may be metaphorically said. I perked up with the assistance of saying to myself: Springboard—get the beat right—keep the hand loose

and flexible—bounce around on a place—go for a
long reach—breathe deeply—do interweavings—
relax—don't go fast until you're ready—let the
hands say where and how to go—be careful—
remember Jimmy—go for an opening chord by
theory—just get started talking—get those shoulders moving—keep that hand from tripping—
they're listening to you—you're playing fast bebop,
lots of interwindings in tight quarters, get especially bebopical—play beautifully—get down on it
—do it.

Little bits and pieces of jazz-handlings showed
themselves to me, and particular nudgings worked
especially in the beginning, as I took notice and
told myself about ways of moving with an instructional nudge 'translated' as a practice, with a quasi-
worded reflexive spark turned right back down into
the keyboard, dissipated as an inner saying into a
singing.

Without getting the beat right, without establishing those prospectivities for articulational
reachings, without assessing the pace-ably available presence of ways for classes of rated traverse,
without essentializing command over these paced
presences in and of the terrain nexus—jazz-handlings did not and cannot appear. For, and I speak
generically here, it don't mean a thing if it ain't got
that swing, and the 'swing' of jazz-handlings was
shored up by express thinking, at first.

But the instruction's express presence, arising from this history, had become situated in the
ways of my hands as: 'Listen carefully to the beats'
is in the ways of the piano tuner's arm and shoulders; 'wait for the dial to return,' an instruction the
young child must noticeably employ, is in the
adult caller's wayful, reconfigurating, sequentially
unfolding hoverings with the telephone; 'be careful
in a typing test' is in the strongly established upright posture; 'reach ahead' is in every undertaken

course of talking—so deeply situated within the ways of my hands had the historically theoretic character of my problematics now become.*

And to say 'remember Jimmy' is a way I have of saying get the time into the fingers, which I can translate as: Keep strong forward prospectivities, get especially bebopical, relax, with a big ETC. I can institute jazz-handlings by telling myself— looking at my hand and composing its appearance in and through play with a posing that satisfies a look which asks—let me see jazz hands.

Telling myself, 'let me see jazz hands,' works as a nudge in that it instructs and notices everything else at the same time. And my instructions

---

*Sociologists speak of a world taken for granted, of a familiar world of everyday life: I lived in a community for many years that was sufficiently small that a single three-digit prefix served, by the permutational possibilities of four remaining numerals, to give everybody in the town a unique phone number. Calling a friend in that community, I dial the opening three digits with an articulational course of traverse whose specific place achievements are encountered through the journey with a familiarity akin to what I find in and through the articulational saying that is the town's name. My hand is just at the edge of almost blurting out these digits, so wordfully of a piece are they, and as the dial returns, a readiness for the next places can almost be impatient in the very wayfulness with which these digits' locations are known.

I find, when calling that town, that over the course of these digits' accomplishment the visual guidance required for employing the device is ever so slightly slackened, a tactile accessibility of this routing making a look at the dial a touch more peripheral than is usual.

When calling a friend who lives high on a hill in that hilly town, from my bedroom in flat Cambridge, Massachusetts, I may have an accompanying image, and find that I am not calling long distance to a place imaged at the other end of the country, via a map picture, or to that hillside town that I may visualize, for example, but am calling up the hill from my long-term residence down the hill.

And in and through the course of the dialing itself, the accompanying image may have, morever, a temporal synchrony where I am in my residence down the hill with a paced presence not unrelated to the pacing of the call, akin to it as, when hearing a song that reminds one of another, the other may be imaged, for example, doing things in time to the music, walking in the fantasy for instance, the time of the music not unaffiliated to the pacing of the recollection.

that work, born of my history as explicitly required |
and consequential noticings, can best be regarded
as a usable compendium of caretaking practices
for toning up, separably usable because each
speaks of all the rest, each another way of saying
the same thing; and now and then doing a 'quick'
saying to myself has useful instigating payoffs in
my current play.

But for the most part I now follow one piece of
advice—heard a long time before from jazz musicians, perhaps their most oft-voiced maxim for
newcomers, literally overheard through my years
of pursuing those notes on the records, regarded
from my standpoint of novice and ethnographer as
nothing but the vaguest of vague talk, accessible
finally as the very detailed talk it was only when a
grasp of the details to which it pointed were themselves accessibly at hand—now my central instruction: SING WHILE YOU ARE PLAYING.

A 'speaking I' is struck by the awesomeness of
finding myself singing as I play, singing right along
with the movements of my fingers, aiming for next
sounds with a synchronous reach of two body
'parts,' an achievement formerly quite impossible.* How am I taking my fingers to places, for it

*With the electric piano, amplifier bypassed, 'real-world
sounds' soaked up by a body-made tape recorder, my ears, so
to plausibly speak (in that, for example, this for-ears device
works to at least soak up that which I can find again as the
music), not 'hearing the sounds'—with this contrivance that
seems initially suggestive nonetheless, and a foot pedal that
can put these sounds into the room and take them away with
a tap on the switch, I play a game.
     Singing aloud, recording my voice, I can see what hap-
pens when these 'ear-ables' are inaccessible (call the music
'soundings,' call these happenings in the air space 'earables').
I may record and compare pitches, reformulating soundings
for the sake of teasing out a possible relevance for production, trying then to quickly abandon the implications of having done a comparison of 'body parts.' A new language would
emerge through such struggles if carried out diligently. Here I
talk loosely, only suggestively, with terms like 'synchrony'
and 'precision' intended only that way.
     With the earables off, the precise correspondence be-
tween the pitches is often thrown into disarray. Hitting the

makes good sense for this I to speak that way (I
reach for a cup just there, ready—set—go, now I
move my arm there), and singing in perfect concert? How do I know what the next notes will sound
like as a joint knowing of voice and fingers, going
there together, not singing along with the fingers,
but singing with the fingers? A speaking I is struck
by the awesomeness of an altogether new coupling, a new hookup, a new organization between
my vocalizations and my fingerings. How is that
done—I take my fingers to places so deeply 'mind-
ful' of what they will sound like that I can sing *at
the same time,* both on the way down into the

switch in the midst of play, for a while I stay in alignment at
times, and then drift off a bit. My singing pitches and fingering pitches will not graphically correspond, on a score, for
example. At times I am very close in the territory so that
graphs would look like a child's handwriting. At times they
look like altogether different signatures. If I use a table, with
ink on my fingertips, measure distances attained there, use
body-made mathematics to define a correspondence, there
are highs where high and lows where low, if I play the game
with serious intent to get the melody done on the table. If I do
fingerings in the air, I find greater discrepancies of differing
orders of disturbance, for playing the game in the air I can
feel that the interdigitations, in not being in contact with their
'missing parts,' are temporally uncertain, for example.

I need to be going to places precisely for that jazz to happen. We have no text here if I cannot find this typewriter terrain being used with impressional contact, and I feel like I am
playing at writing if I type in the air. The home territory makes
it possible to not need the eyeables to be certain, their use
mainly required not to detect errors but to keep the margins
right, though the skilled typist often reaches for a return key
or lever with 'margin-proper' pacing, and without looking
(and without needing the signal bell).

If that jazz on the records could arise as 'home-territory
playing,' particular digit-key responsibilities never changing,
various losses of synchrony would be minimized. But should
I venture beyond a way essentially at hand, adventure beyond
a blues scale, for example, I *may* lose synchronous touch. In
adventurous play I often reach for a note without knowing
what it will sound like (without being synchronously aimed
with fingers and singings), and then proceed wayfully along,
having 'locked in.' With earables not available, such adven-
tures often slip from synchronous alignment.

Standing outside the circumstances of play I find that
having the earables serves to sustain a continual centered-

terrain, these piano pitches. Are the singings I do merely given to me as some payoff to keep me engrossed, my fingers operating through independent mechanisms beyond my awareness? Am I really singing along behind the sounds at a rapid rate, with a differential lag in timing I do not notice, some split-second 'neurological' delay? Is an overwhelming impression of the jointly aimed singing of a unidirectional and multilaterally influenced body an illusion of ignorance about my real work-

---

ness, a synchrony of singings and fingerings. While my hands may be wayfully and securely targeted along essentialized routings, the sound-there-routing hand, ambiguously linked with my vocalizations without the earables' presence, is not of a singing body knowing where it is going and going there together.

And the pitches, so-called, are distanced placings in, for, and of the body, and the 'earability' issues applies to place achievements generically speaking. The notion that some languages are nonsemantic with respect to pitch or tone is an artificial observation, based on a productionally unwarranted differentiation of 'aspects' of talking and an unexplicated assumption of what pitch or tone are in music making as the contrastive model. I conceive talking to be paced-place achievings. If any thing is semantic, available for semantics in co-bodied movings, it is sustained articulational courses from place to place, each next place to each next, just here, just there, for us together.

In my opinion, a productional distinction between melodying and saying is not empirically justifiable (however a 'use theory' could specify rather massive social organizational differences). Until we allow that music 'talks about itself,' in no other sense than we must allow that this course of movements that I do—about, is a course of movements in language's talking about itself—confusions remain. And of course the question cannot even be clearly put by a 'language' that considers itself privileged to ask such questions. This claim is not intended as an observation immune from that paradox, which would be self-contradictory. My interests here, as all interests, are essentially and irremediably confined by this so-called reflexive inescapability, which, however, is not a methodological dead end, but a beginning for defining the scope and possibilities of rational inquiry. Can we sketch an orchestration of descriptive writings that seems to more closely 'point to' possibilities for the study of bodily activities, in terms of which such inquiry might receive a mundane grounding in accounts of accomplished paced-place achievings?

ings? And my sayings themselves—are they too a token of some sort for the real happenings?

I choose places to go, in what this speaking I finds as miraculous ways, miraculous merely against the background of my history with the piano, and a history of other speakings that seem to leave little room for a conception that would not partitionalize 'my' body in some way (This history simultaneously reconstructs doings to render them into a form for close study, contributing to as it derives warrant from such partitionalizing.)

From an upright posture I look down at my hands on the piano keyboard during play, with a look that is hardly a look at all. But standing back I find that I proceed through and in a terrain nexus, doing singings with my fingers, so to speak, a single voice at the tips of the fingers, going for each next note in sayings just now and just then, just this soft and just this hard, just here and just there, with definiteness of aim throughout, taking my fingers to places, so to speak, and being guided, so to speak. I sing with my fingers, so to speak, and only so to speak, for there is a new 'I' that the speaking I gestures toward with a pointing at the music that says: It is a singing body and this I (here, too, so to speak) sings.

Bibliography

My book's relationship to an extant literature on music making, the body, problems of oriented space and time, and kindred issues, is essentially tangential. This is not to say that others have not written about questions directly related to topics that have emerged in my efforts to learn jazz play; an extensive bibliography of writings from various disciplines could be assembled. It is to say that there is a fundamental difference in perspective between most available studies of conduct and that from which my observations derive.

The psychologist Lashley's work on the problem of serial order in behavior is perhaps closely related to the substance of issues I confronted at the piano. But Harvey Sacks's early conjectures on how the policeman detects trouble, against the background of the perceptibly normal features of the environment of his beat, or his later efforts to warrant relevant observations about conversation by appeal to what conversationalists themselves display as relevant—such studies are more to the point as a source of perspective.

I have taken my directions here from the keyboard, rather intentionally avoiding consultation with a causally motivated literature on objective structures of 'tempo,' 'tactility,' 'neuromuscular' coordination, and the like. My concern has been description, not explanation, my task to see if close details of the ways of the hand, known to their possessor in the context of striving for a normatively organized course of doings, could be developed. As I worked at the keyboard, as that jazz heard on records came into actual view, I sought a descriptive account of these ways, free from psychological imputation and neuroanatomical theorizing. And in that respect my perspective is phenomenological in motive, ethnographic in origin, and definitional in intent. It seeks to advance upon those essentially programmatic writings that argue the necessity for close studies of so-called embodied conduct, by offering a first sample of what a productionally situated account might look like.

I should like to ask you to treat this account as an approach toward a *definition* of jazz music as the hands' ways. If there is to be the phenomenon of 'jazz music' to explore (or any other phenomenon of social action), for others to write of and analyze, for psychology, history, philosophy, linguistics, sociology, biology, musicology, and the rest, first there must be its production. How must the 'is-ness' of this conduct, its 'quiddity'—to use Harold Garfinkel's favored term—be established as the definitive ground for further descriptive inquiry?

I treat the 'actor's perspective' as definitionally critical for the initial specification of this quiddity, for establishing the 'what' of social action, to which all accounts must be addressed. This is not a question of argument; it is a statement of program. And the task then becomes making that specification as richly detailed as possible, as a definitional effort. I have sought to delineate the jazz musician's practical accomplishment, inspected and described, in Merleau-Ponty's terms, with 'no body but himself to consult.' And I have tried to implant 'consciousness' or 'subjectivity' in the real-world doings and looks of these hands at work. My description is meant to be a guide to the looks of improvisatory hands. If it informs those looks and does so in detail, offering, from among the many 'things' to be seen, affairs that should be noticed, then a 'subjective standpoint' grounded in the problematics of a concrete task may pave the way for the intersubjective pursuit of warrantable structures of action.

The brief list of writings below furnishes a background of sociological and philosophical writings in which I found a productional perspective emerging. These works served as a point of departure, but when I turned to the piano I had to put them aside (as they in principle ask to be put aside) and let the tasks of moving through the keyboard dictate topics and questions to pursue.

Garfinkel, Harold. *Studies in Ethnomethodology* (Englewood Cliffs, N. J.: Prentice-Hall, 1967).
——— "Collected Papers," forthcoming.
Gurwitsch, Aron. *The Field of Consciousness* (Pittsburgh: Duquesne University Press, 1964).
Husserl, Edmund. *Logical Investigations* (London: Routledge and Kegan Paul, 1970)
——— *Ideas* (New York: Collier Books, 1962).
Merleau-Ponty, Maurice. *The Structure of Behavior* (Boston: Beacon Press, 1963).
——— *The Phenomenology of Perception* (London: Routledge and Kegan, 1962).
Sacks, Harvey. "Unpublished Lecture Notes" (University of California, Irvine, 1968-1974).
Schutz, Alfred. *Collected Papers,* 1-3 (The Hague: Martinus Nijhoff, 1962, 1964, 1966).

Straus, Erwin. *Phenomenological Psychology* (New York: Basic Books, 1966).

Sudnow, David, ed. *Studies in Social Interaction* (New York: Free Press, 1972).

Turner, Roy, ed. *Ethnomethodology* (Baltimore: Penguin Books, 1974).